973

AMERICAN HERITAGE
ILLUSTRATED HISTORY
OF THE UNITED STATES

VOLUME 19

INDEX
AND BIBLIOGRAPHY

LIBRARY EDITION

SILVER BURDETT PRESS, INC.
1989

5 6 4 3

Library of Congress Catalog Card Number: ~~89-50419~~ 89 - 73399
ISBN 0-382-09877-3 (Vol. 19)
ISBN 0-382-09878-1 (Set)

This 1989 revised edition is published and distributed by Silver Burdett Press, Inc., Prentice-Hall Building, Englewood Cliffs, NJ 07632
by arrangement with American Heritage, a division of Forbes, Inc.

Manufactured in the United States of America

CONTENTS OF THE COMPLETE SERIES

Editor's Note to the Revised Edition
Introduction by ALLAN NEVINS
Main text by ROBERT G. ATHEARN

Vol. 1   THE NEW WORLD
Special picture portfolios:
THE SPANISH CONQUEST
THE PILGRIMS' EUROPE
Special contributor: THOMAS F. MCGANN — THE
ORDEAL OF CABEZ DE VACA

Vol. 2   COLONIAL AMERICA
Special picture portfolios:
THE FRENCH AND INDIAN WARS
LIFE IN COLONIAL AMERICA
Special contributor:
A.L. ROWSE — THE PILGRIM AND PURITAN FATHERS

Vol. 3   THE REVOLUTION
Special picture portfolios:
THE DECLARATION OF INDEPENDENCE
THE ARMS AND THE MEN
Special contributor:
GEORGE F. SCHEER—
FRANCIS MARION: THE ELUSIVE SWAMP FOX

Vol. 4   A NEW NATION
Special picture portfolios:
THOMAS JEFFERSON
THE WAR AT SEA
Special contributor:
OLIVER JENSEN — THE MANY-FACETED MR. PEALE

Vol. 5   YOUNG AMERICA
Special picture portfolios:
STIRRINGS OF INDUSTRY
NEW ROADS—THE WATERWAYS
Special contributor:
ARNOLD WHITRIDGE—
ELI WHITNEY: NEMESIS OF THE SOUTH

Vol. 6   THE FRONTIER
Special picture portfolios:
THE GREAT GOLD RUSH
INDIANS OF THE PLAINS
Special contributor:
STEPHEN W. SEARS—
JEDEDIAH S. SMITH: UNSUNG PATHFINDER OF THE WEST

Vol. 7   WAR WITH MEXICO
Special picture portfolios:
WAR IN THE WEST
WHALERS AND CLIPPERS
Special contributor:
GERALD W. JOHNSON—
DANIEL WEBSTER: GREAT MAN ELOQUENT

Vol. 8   THE CIVIL WAR
Special picture portfolios:
PRESIDENT LINCOLN
THE NAVAL WAR
Special contributor:
BRUCE CATTON — "HAYFOOT, STRAWFOOT!"

Vol. 9   WINNING THE WEST
Special picture portfolios:
COWBOYS—LIFE ON THE RANGE
THE LAST WAR WITH THE INDIANS
Special contributor:
STEWART H. HOLBROOK — THE LEGEND OF JIM HILL

Vol. 10   AGE OF STEEL
Special picture portfolios:
MAKE WAY FOR THE IRON HORSE!
THE ROBBER BARONS
Special contributor:
JOHN GARRATY — WILLIAM JENNINGS BRYAN

Vol. 11   THE GILDED AGE
Special picture portfolios:
THE ROMANTIC WORLD OF CURRIER AND IVES
THE VICTORIAN LOOK
Special contributor:
NELSON LANSDALE — MRS. GARDNER AND HER PALACE

Vol. 12   A WORLD POWER
Special picture portfolios:
THE SPANISH-AMERICAN WAR
THE CITY GOES MODERN
Special contributor:
ROBERT L. HEILBRONER—
ANDREW CARNEGIE: EPITAPH FOR THE STEELMASTER

Vol. 13   WORLD WAR I
Special picture portfolios:
THE WAR IN THE AIR
AMERICA AS ADVERTISED
Special contributor:
ALLAN NEVINS — HENRY FORD: A COMPLEX MAN

Vol. 14   THE ROOSEVELT ERA
Special picture portfolios:
F.D.R
THE ARTIST'S AMERICA
Special contributor:
MERLO J. PUSEY — F.D.R VS. THE SUPREME COURT

Vol. 15   WORLD WAR II
Special picture portfolios:
D-DAY
THE UNITED NATIONS
Special contributor:
ONE WHO SURVIVED:
THE NARRATIVE OF ALLEN HEYN

Vol. 16   DECADES OF COLD WAR
Special picture portfolios:
REVOLUTION IN AMERICAN ART
THAT'S ENTERTAINMENT
Special contributor:
WILLIAM T. LEUCHTENBURG — JFK 20 YEARS LATER

Vol. 17   THE VIETNAM ERA
Special picture portfolios:
VIETNAM: THE WAR IN COLOR
THE WORLD OF OUTER SPACE
Special contributor:
WALTER KARP—
LOOKING BACK ON WATERGATE: THE HOUR OF THE FOUNDERS

Vol. 18   AMERICA TODAY
Special picture portfolios:
THE NEW CHINA
AMERICA CELEBRATES
Special contributor:
RICHARD B. MORRIS—
A FEW PARCHMENT PAGES TWO HUNDRED YEARS LATER

EACH VOLUME CONTAINS AN ENCYCLOPEDIC SECTION; MASTER INDEX IN VOLUME 19

CONTENTS OF VOLUME 19

INDEX

Note: Page references are to volume number:page number (e.g., **3**:200 means Volume 3, page 200). References to pages in the encyclopedic section at the back of each volume are indicated by the letter **E**. **Boldface** page numbers indicate an extended discussion of that topic. *Italic* page numbers refer to photos, illustrations, and/or their captions. The word *map* appears in parentheses after each map reference.

A

Aaron, Henry Louis, **18E:632,** *632*

Abolitionist movement, **6:491–93, 6E:188,** *188,* 193, 199, 203, 207; **7:554–57,** 587–88; **9E:**300

Abortion, **18E:662**

Abstract expressionism, **16:**1365, **16E:558**

Acadia, **2E:40,** *40*

Acheson, Dean, **16E:558–59,** *558*

Acres of Diamonds, **11:**962–63

Act Concerning Religion (1649), **2:**99

Adair, James, **2E:40**

Adams, Charles Francis, **7:**611, **7E:225,** *225*; **10:**825

Adams, Franklin Pierce, **13E:447**

Adams, Henry Brooks, **11E:373**

Adams, John, **2:**158, *161,* **2E:42,** 62; **3:**190, *192,* 193, 245, 247, **3E:93,** 108; **4:**280–81, 301–2, **4E:114,** *114*
  as President, **4:313–16**

Adams, John Quincy, **5:**366, 376, **5E:151,** *151*
  Monroe Doctrine and, **5:**369
  as president, **5:391–93,** *392*

Adams, Samuel, **2:**156, *163,* 164, 165, **2E:40,** 42, 44, 47; **3:**185, 189, 190, *246,* **3E:**84, 88, 91, 109

Adamson Act, **12E:410**

Adams-Onis Treaty, **5:**366, **5E:151–52**

Addams, Jane, **11:***945,* 946, **11E:373–74,** *373*; **12:**1055

Adena, **1E:24**

Adenauer, Conrad, **16:***1436*

Advertising in 1920s, **13E:***1135–45*

AEC (Atomic Energy Commission), **15E:538; 16E:**580–81

Affirmative action, **18:**1549

Afghanistan, **18:**1545

AFL (American Federation of Labor), **10:**829, **10E:337,** 351; **12:**1053; **13:**1131–32, **13E:461;** **14:**1223–24, **14E:500**

AFL-CIO (American Federation of Labor-Congress of Industrial Organizations), **16E:558,** 577, 578, 583

Africa, **1:**20
  in World War II, **15:**1296–97, *1303* (map)

African National Congress (ANC), **18E:664**

Agassiz, Louis, **5E:152–53,** *152*

Agent Orange, **17E:595**

Age of Reason, **4:**275

Agnew, Spiro T., **17:***1473,* 1475, 1479, 1481–82, *1481,* **17E:595–96,** *595*

Agricultural Adjustment Act (1933), **14:**1185

Agricultural Adjustment Act (1936), **14:**1240

Agricultural Adjustment Act (1938), **14:**1246

Agricultural Adjustment Administration (AAA), **14:**1239–40

Agricultural Marketing Act of 1929, **13:**1130–31

Agriculture, **3:***249*; **4:**276; **5:**423, 435; **8:***700;* **9:**766–69, 800; **10:***844,* **845–60,** 892–93
  early 20th century, **12:**1059
  in 1920s, **13:**1129–31, **13E:477; 14:**1176
  in 1930s, **14:**1185, *1218–22,* 1219, 1239, 1246–47, 1250; **15E:539**
  in 1980s, **18E:643–44**
  Civil War and, **8:**698
  irrigation, **9:**770, 774; **10:**845
  land legislation, **10:845–47**
  mechanization of, **5:***384–85,* **443–48; 8:**700; **10:**848; **12:**1059; **13:**1131
  overproduction in, **10:**850–51
  prairie politics and, **10:853–60**
    populists, **10:855–60**
  railroads and, **5:**441; **10:**852–53, *853*
  technological advances in, **5:***384–85,* **5E:170–71,** *170*; **10:**847–49, *848*
  in underdeveloped countries, **17E:598**
  the West and, **5:**435
  see also Cowboys; Farmers; Plantations

Agriculture, Department of, **14:**1239

Aguinaldo, Emilio, **12:**1009, **12E:410,** *410*

AIDS (Acquired Immune Deficiency Syndrome), **18:**1575, **18E:632**

AIM (American Indian Movement), **17E:596**

Air brakes, railroad, **10:**821, 849, **10E:369–70**

Airplanes, 12:1059–60, 12E:414
  see also Air warfare; Aviation
Air warfare
  Vietnam War, 17:*1466–67*
  World War I, 13:*1105–17*
  World War II, 15:*1284–85*, 1306
Aix-la-Chapelle, Treaty of (1748), 2:132
Alabama claims, 9E:299
Alamo, the, 7:*562–63*
Alaska, 2E:43
  purchase of, 9E:299
Albany Plan of Union, 2E:40–41, 3:253
Albee, Edward, 16:1399
Alcott, (Amos) Bronson, 6E:188
Alden, John, 1E:32; 2E:41, *41*
Alder Gulch, 9:736
Aldrich, Nelson W., 10:*870*, 10E:336
Aldrin, Edwin, Jr., 17:*1479, 1494, 1496, 1497, 1499*
Alexander I, 5:365–66, 5E:152
Alger, Horatio, 11:963, *963*
Algeria, War with, 4E:115–16, *116*
Algonquians, 1:74
  see also Pequot
Ali, Muhammad, 17E:596, *596*
Alien and Sedition Acts of 1798, 4:314, 316; 5:398;
  18:1589
Allen, Ethan, 3E:77
Allen, Frederick Lewis, 13E:447
Allison, William B., 10:884, 10E:336
Allouez, Claude Jean, 2E:41
Almagro, Diego de, 1E:3
Almagro the Lad, 1E:3
Altgeld, John Peter, 10:830, 10E:336–37, *336*
Alvarado, Hernando de, 1E:3
Ambrister, Robert, 5:366, 5E:153
Amendments to the Constitution, *see* Bill of
    Rights; *and specific amendments (e.g.,*
    Fourteenth Amendment)
America Firsters, 15:1270
American Academy of Arts and Sciences, 3E:80
American Colonization Society, 6:491–92,
    6E:188–89
American Expeditionary Force, 13E:447–48, *447*
  see also World War I
American Express, 9E:332
American Federation of Labor (AFL), 10:829,
    10E:337, 351; 12:1053; 13:1131–32, 13E:461;
    14:1223–24, 14E:500
American Federation of Labor-Congress of Indus-
    trial Organizations (AFL-CIO), 16E:558,
    577, 578, 583
American Indian Movement (AIM), 17E:596
American Peace Society, 6E:189
American Philosophical Society, 4:297, 4E:114–15
American Protective Association, 10:887, 10E:337
American Railway Union, 10:*827–29*, 830
American Red Cross, 9E:300

American Revolution, 3E:77–111
  causes of, 2:151–69
    Boston Massacre, 2:*160*, 162–64, 2E:44
    Boston Tea Party, 2:*168*, 169, 2E:44, *44*
    Currency Act, 2:155
    Marion's operations, 3:*262* (map)
    Navigation Acts, 2:151–52, 2E:43, 62
    Quartering Act, 2:155–56
    Revenue Act, 2:161
    Revere's ride, 3E:*103* (map)
    Stamp Act, 2:*154*, 155, 156, *157*, 158–59, 161,
      2E:67–68, *67, 68*; 3E:89
    Sugar Act, 2:*153*, 155, 156, 2E:68–69, *69*
    Townshend Acts, 2:161, 164–65, 2E:69
  climax of, 3:220–23
  Declaration of Independence, 3:190–93,
      197–208, 254, 3E:85, *85*
  equipment and uniforms, 3:*228–41*
  financing of, 3E:99–100, 105
  first American victories in, 3:213–14, 217
  France and, 3:195–96, 220–22, *222–23, 240–41*,
      264, 3E:81, 84, 94–95, 97, 103–4
  government and, 3:256–57
  guerrilla warfare and, 3:261–68, 3E:97, 105, 106
  Hessians and, 3:212, 214, *240*
  Indians and, 3E:80, 81, 105, 106
  land distribution and, 3:247–50
  loyalists and, 3:189, 193–94, 248–49, 3E:93,
      97–98; 4:281
  naval war, 3:223–26, *224–25*, 3E:79, 85–86, 91–94
  political and economic life after, 3:245–54,
      256–57
  Popular Party and, 3:194
  propaganda and, 3:189, 194–96, 3E:101
  settlement of, 3:221–23, 226, 3E:107
  social class and, 3:193–94, 247–50
  southern campaign, 3:210–11, 261–67, 3E:97
  Spain and, 3:195, 196, 221
  strategy of, 3:196, 209–23, 261–68, 3E:78
  taxation and, 3E:80–81
  see also Continental Army; *specific battles and
      leaders*
American Sugar Refining Company, 10:826
American Temperance Union, 6E:189
American Woman Suffrage Association, 11E:392
Ames, Fisher, 4:284, 309, 4E:115
Amherst, Maj. Gen. Jeffrey, 2:*117*, 2E:41
Amistad case, 5E:152–53
Amnesty International, 18E:632–33
Amory, John, 2:*144*
Anabaptists, 1:56
Anarchists, *see* Goldman, Emma
Anders, William A., 17E:597
Anderson, John B., 18E:633
Anderson, Robert, 7E:225
Anderson, Maj. Robert, 7:*618*, 618, 619
Anderson, Sherwood, 13E:448

Andersonville, **8E:262,** *262*

Andŕe, John, **3E:77,** *71*

Andros, Sir Edmund, **2:**102, *102,* **2E:41,** 48, 49

Anglican Church, **2:**97; **3:**250

Anne, Queen of England, **2:***126*

Antarctica, **14E:**487–88

Anthony, Susan B., **9E:299–300,** *299;* **11E:**392

Antietam, Battle of, **8:645–46,** *646*

Antifederalists, **4:**290, 309, 310

   see also Democratic-Republicans

Anti-Nebraska, **7:**557

Anti-Semitism, Holocaust and, **16E:570**

Antiwar movement, *see* Vietnam War, antiwar
    movement

Anza, Juan Bautista de, **2E:41–42**

Anzio, **15:**1301

Apaches, **9:**797, **9E:**317–18

Apalache, **1:**83

Apartheid, **18E:663–64**

Apollo space program, **17:***1494–1500,* 1503,
    17E:596–97, *597;* **18:**1539

Apple computer, **17:**1507

Appleseed, Johnny, **6E:**197

Aquino, Corazon Cojuangco, **18E:633–34**

Arabella, **2E:42**

Arapahoes, **9:**792, 796, **3E:**307

Arbella, **2:**174, 176, **2E:45**

Arbuthnot, Alexander, **5:**366

Arbuthnot-Ambrister affair, **5:**366, **5E:153**

Architecture, **9E:**326–27, **14E:**517–18

   late 19th century, **11:**973, *974–75,* 976, **11E:**387,
    389, 393–94, 400

    Jefferson and, **4:***294–95, 298–99;* **5E:**170

   see also individual architects

Arctic, the, **14E:**487

Ardennes, **15:**1304

Arias Sanchez, Oscar, **18:**1569, **18E:**658

Aristocracy (the Four Hundred), **12:1050–52**

Arms, *see* Weapons

Arms control and disarmament, **18:**1539, 1544,
    1545, **1571–73**

   Eighteen-Nation Disarmament Committee
    (ENDC), **16E:**580

   Intermediate Nuclear Forces (INF) Treaty,
    18:1571, 1573; **18E:650**

   SALT (Strategic Arms Limitation Talks),
    17:1478, **17E:**624–25

   SALT II, **18:**1545

   START (Strategic Arms Reduction Talks),
    18E:650

   Washington Conference for the Limitation of Ar-
    mament (1921–1922), **13:**1123, 1133–34

   World Disarmament Conference (1932),
    14:1215–16

Armstrong, Neil A., **17:***1479,* 1492, *1494, 1497,*
    1499

Army, U.S., **9:**739, 791

Army-McCarthy hearings, **16:**1391, **16E:**577

Arnold, Benedict, **3:**209, *211,* 217, *216–17,*
    3E:77–78, *78*

Arnold, Jack, **9E:**312

Aroostook War, **6E:189**

Art

   19th century, **6E:**192–93, 196–97, 222

   late 19th century, **11:972–73; 979–88**

   in 1930s, **14:**1221–23, *1227–38*

   1940s-1960s, **16:***1365–83,* **16E:**558

   abstract expressionism, **16:**1365, **16E:**558

   advertising, in 1920s, **13:***1135–45*

   Ash Can School of painting, **14E:**1221–22

   New York School, **16:**1365

   see also individual artists

Arthur, Chester Alan, **10:**878, **10E:337–38,** *337*

Arthur, Timothy Shay, **6E:189**

Articles of Confederation, **3:254–57, 3E:78–79;**
    4:276, 284–86, 289

Ashby, Turner, **8E:**262

Ash Can School of painting, **14:**1221–22

Ashley, William Henry, **6E:189–90**

Astor, John Jacob, **6:**514, *517,* **6E:190**

Astrolabe, **1E:3**

Atahualpa, **1:***21,* **1E:3,** *3*

Atchison, Topeka & Santa Fe Railroad, **10:**821

Atkinson, Gen. Henry, **6E:**193

Atlanta, siege of, **8:***679,* 679, 680, 683–84

Atlantic cable, **11E:**381–82

Atlantic Charter, **15E:521,** *521*

Atomic bomb, **15E:**551; **16:**1385

   Manhattan Project, **14E:**500; **15E:537–38,** *537;*
    16E:580

Atomic Energy Commission (AEC), **15E:**538;
    16E:580–81

Attlee, Clement Richard, **15:**1335, **15E:521–22**

Attucks, Crispus, **2E:42,** 42

audiencia, **1:**43

Audubon, John James, **5E:153,** *153*

Austin, Moses, **6:**518, **6E:190**

Austin, Stephen Fuller, **6:**518–19, *521,* **6E:190–91,**
    190

Austria (Austria-Hungary), **2:**127; **13:**1085;
    14:1179; **15:**1266

Austrian Succession, War of the, *see* King
    George's War

Automated production, **17:**1510

Automobiles, **12:***1042–43,* **1057–59,** *1059,* **12E:**417,
    417; **14:**1209; **18:**1562

Aviation, **17:***1512*

   Lindbergh, **14E:501–2**

   Wiley Post, **14E:507–8**

   sound barrier, **16E:**587

   women in, **14E:**492; **16E:**587

   Wright brothers, **12:**1060, *1062–63,* **12E:444,**
    444

   see also Airplanes; Air warfare

Aztecs, **1:**26, 26, *27–31, 33–35,* 34, *39,* **1E:3–4,** 10, 24, 29, 34–35

B

Babcock, Orville E., **8:**707, **8E:262–63**
Baby M. Case, **18E:634–35,** *635*
"Back to Africa" movement, **13E:459**
Bacon's Rebellion, **2E:42–43**
Badoglio, Marshal Pietro, **15:**1297
Bagot, Sir Charles, **5:**365, **5E:153**
Bainbridge, William, **4E:115**
Baker, Howard, **18E:635–36**
Baker, Newton D., **13:**1094, **13E:448**
Baker, Ray Stannard, **12E:410**
Bakke, Allen, **18:**1549
Balance of terror, **16:**1394
Balboa, Vasco Nuñez de, **1:**19, 38, **1E:4–5,** *4*
Baltimore, Lord, **2:**99, 104, 105
Baltimore (Maryland), colonial, **2:***140*
Baltimore & Ohio (B&O) railroad, **5:***439;* **10:**828
Bancroft, George, **6E:191,** *191*
Bank, national, **4:**306, 309; **5:400–2, 5E:163**
  see also Bank of the United States
Bank holiday (1933), **14:**1182
Bank of the United States, **5:**154, *400,* **400–2,** *402*
  Jackson and, **5:**401–2
  Second, **5E:171**
Banks, **10:**868–69
  in 1930s, **14:**1178, 1182–83
Banks, Nathaniel Prentiss, **8E:263**
Bannach (Montana), gold rush in, **9:**735–37, 740
Banneker, Benjamin, **4E:115**
Baptists, **3:**250
Barbary Wars, **4:***322,* **4E:115–16,** *116* (map)
Barbed wire, **9:**770, *771,* 772; **10E:350–51**
Baring, Alexander, **7E:225–26**
Barlow, Joel, **4E:116–17**
Barnard, Christiaan, **17:**1513
Barnard, Henry, **6:**495, **6E:191–92**
Barnum, Phineas T., **6:***488–89,* **6E:192,** *192;* **11:**940, *942*
Barry, Capt. John, **3:**224, **3E:79**
Barry, William Taylor, **5:**394, **5E:153–54**
Barton, Clara, **9E:300,** *300*
Bartram, John, **2E:43**
Baruch, Bernard M., **13:**1094–95, **13E:448–49,** *449*
Baruch Plan, **13E:449**
Baseball, **11:***936, 937,* 939–40, **11E:381;** **18E:632**
Bates, Edward, **7:**611, **7E:226**
Battle Hymn of the Republic, **8E:280**
Bay of Pigs invasion, **16:**1434, **16E:559**
Beard, Charles A., **1:**63
Beauregard, Gen. Pierre Gustave Toutant, **7:***618,* 618–19, **7E:226,** *226*
Beckwourth, James P., **6E:192**

Beecher, Henry Ward, **7:**557, **7E:226–27,** *227;* **11:**914–18, *915,* **11E:392**
Beecher Island fight, **9:***782–83*
Beer and Wine Revenue Act (1922), **14:**1217–18
Begin, Menachem, **18:**1544–45
Beirut, bombing of Marine compound in, **18:**1564–65
Belgium, **13:**1102, **15:**1268
Belknap, William North, **8:**707, **8E:263**
Bell, Alexander Graham, **10:**818, *822,* **10E:338**
Bell, John, **7:**609, 611, **7E:227**
Bellamy, Edward, **10:**826; **11E:374–75**
Belleau Wood, Battle of, **13:***1095*
Bellow, Saul, **18E:636**
Bellows, George Wesley, **11:***944–45;* **13E:449**
Benjamin, Judah Philip, **8E:263–64**
Bennett, Floyd, **14E:487**
Bennett, James Gordon, **7E:227;** **11:**937, 938
Bennett, James Gordon, Jr., **11:**909, **11E:375**
Benteen, Capt. Frederick, **9E:308–9,** 326
Benton, Thomas Hart, **5:**400, **5E:154,** *154;* **6:**517; **13:***1133;* **14:***1238,* **14E:484,** *484*
Berenson, Bernard, **11E:383**
Beria, Lavrenti P., **16:**1392–93
Bering, Vitus, **2E:43**
Berkeley, Lord John, **2:**103, **2E:43,** 46, 47
Berkeley, Sir William, **2E:43,** *43,* 42–43, 46
Berle, Adolf A., Jr., **14:**1239, **14E:486**
Berlin, **16:**1418
  blockade and airlift (1948–49), **16:**1362, **16E:559–60**
Berlin Wall, **16:**1418
Bernard, Sir Francis, **2:**158, **2E:43–44,** *44*
Bernstein, Carl, **17:**1480
Bethune, Mary McLeod, **16E:560,** *560*
Bicentennial, the, **18:**1539–40, *1577–79*
Bicycles, **12:***1068*
Biddle, Nicholas, **5:***400,* 401–2, *402,* **5E:154**
Bierce, Ambrose Gwinett, **12E:410–11**
Bierstadt, Albert, **6E:192–93**
Big business, *see* Monopolies; Trusts
Bilbo, Theodore Gilmore, **15E:522,** *522*
Bill of Rights, **2E:54;** **3E:96;** **4:**302, 304, **4E:117;** **18:**1592–93
Billy the Kid, **9E:300–1,** *301*
Bimini, **1E:28**
Bingham, George Caleb, **5E:154–55**
Birmingham (Alabama), civil-rights movement in, **16:**1422, **16E:562**
Birney, James Gillespie, **6:**493, **6E:193**
Bishop, Billy, **13:***1116*
Bismarck, Otto von, **13E:479**
Bismarck Sea, Battle of the, **15:**1300
Black, Hugo LaFayette, **14:**1258, **14E:484,** *485*
Black Bart (Charley Boles), **9E:332**
Black codes, **8E:268**
Blackfoot Indians, **6:**507
Black Friday, **10:**865, **10E:338–39,** *339*

Black Hawk, Chief, **6E:193**
Black Hawk War, **6E:193**
Black Hills Exploring and Mining Association, **9:738**
Black Kettle, **9:**780, 781, 785, 792, 794, **9E:301**
Black Muslims, **16E:562**
Black nationalism, **17E:601**
  Garvey and, **13E:459–60**
Blackout of 1965, **17E:597**
Blacks, **11:912–13**
  in 1960s, **17:1450,** 1453–54
  in 1970s, **18:1552**
  affirmative action, **18:1549**
  American Colonization Society and, **6E:188–89**
  American Revolution and, **2E:**42; **3:**264
  "Back to Africa" movement, **13E:459**
  Buffalo soldiers, **9E:302**
  busing, **17E:599**
  Carter administration and, **18:1547**
  in Civil War, **8E:287–88,** 287
  in colonial America, **2:**146
  as cowboys, **9E:322–23**
  education of, **11E:404**
  housing, **16:1420**
  Ku Klux Klan and, **8:707**
  race riots, **17:**1450, 1453–54
  Reconstruction and, **8:**710–11, 711
  Scottsboro boys case, **14E:510–11,** 510
  Seminoles and, **5E:179**
  Social Darwinism and, **11:963–64**
  in sports, **16E:584**
    baseball, **18E:632**
  voting rights of, **8:**703–4, 706
  women, **16E:560**
    in literature, **3E:110**
  see also Civil rights; Civil Rights Act; Civil-rights movement; Segregation; Slavery
Black Thursday, **14E:485**
Black Tuesday, **14E:485**
Blaine, James G., **10E:339; 11:910–13,** 911; **12:996**
Blair, Francis P., **5E:155,** 155
Bland, Richard Parks, **10:884, 10E:339–40**
Bland-Allison Act, **10:885, 10E:340**
Blennerhassett, Harman, **4E:117**
Blizzards, **9:**772, 773
  of 1888, **9E:301**
Bloomer, Amelia Jenks, **6:491,** 493, **6E:193**
Blues music, **12E:420**
Bly, Nellie, see Cochrane, Elizabeth
Bodmer, Carl, **5E:155**
Boelcke, Oswald, **13:**1106, 1116
Boleyn, Anne, **1E:17**
Bolivia, **1:**32–33
Bond, Julian, **17E:597–98,** 598
B-1 bomber, **18:1545**
Bonhomme Richard, **3:**224, 224–25, **3E:79**
Bonnie and Clyde, **13E:449**

Bonus Army (Bonus Expeditionary Force), **14:**1179, **14E:486,** 486
Books, see Literature
Boone, Daniel, **3:**251; **6:**454, **6E:194,** 194
Booth, Edwin, **11E:375–76,** 375
Booth, John Wilkes, **8:**662, 663, 684, **8E:264,** 264
Borah, William E., **13:1104; 13E:450; 14:1257**
Borden, Lizzie Andrew, **9E:301–2,** 301
Border Ruffians, **7:**556, 557
Bork, Robert H., **17:1483; 18:1575**
Borlaug, Norman Ernest, **17E:598**
Borman, Frank, **17E:597**
Boston, colonial, **2:**141, 156
Boston Massacre, **2:**160, 162–64, **2E:44**
Boston Tea Party, **2:**168, 169, **2E:44,** 44
Bourke-White, Margaret, **14E:488**
Bow, Clara, **13:**1158, 1159, **13E:450**
Bowdoin, James, **3E:79–80; 4:**282
Bowie, James, **7E:227–28**
Boxer Rebellion, **12:**1030–31, 1032, **12E:411,** 411
Boxing, **11E:399–400**
Bozeman, Montana, **9E:302**
Bozeman Trail, **9:**792–93, 796, **9E:302**
Braddock, Edward, **2:**111–13, **2E:44–45,** 45
Bradford, William, **1:**54, **1E:27; 2:**173–74, **2E:45**
Bradley, Joseph P., **8E:264–65**
Bradley, Omar Nelson, **15E:522–23,** 523
Bradstreet, Anne, **2E:45**
Brady, James Buchanan ("Diamond Jim"), **11E:376**
Brady, Mathew B., **8E:265,** 265
Bragg, Braxton, **8:**645–47, 649, 672, 672, 673, 674–75, 676, **8E:265–66**
Brain Trust, **14E:486–87**
Bramah, Joseph, **5:**447, **5E:155**
Brandeis, Louis D., **14:**1254, 1256, **14E:487**
Brandeis Brief, **14E:487**
Brandt, Willy, **16:**1436
Brannan, Sam, **6:**469, 471, **6E:194**
Brant, Joseph, **3E:80**
Brazil, **1:**19, 20
Brebeuf, Jean de, **1E:5**
Breckinridge, John C., **7:**609, 611, **7E:228**
Breed's Hill, see Bunker Hill, Battle of
Brendan, Saint, **1E:5**
Brest-Litovsk, Treaty of, **13:1094**
Brewster, Elder, **2:**171, 173
Brewster, William, **1:**49, 55, 58; **2:**173, **2E:45–46**
Brezhnev, Leonid, **18:**1539, 1545, **18E:636–37**
Briand, Aristide, **13E:466**
Bridger, James ("Jim"), **6:**514, 517, **6E:194–95,** 194
Britain, Battle of (1940), **15:1268**
British Guiana, **12:996**
Broadway musical, **16:**1396–97
Brock, Sir Isaac, **4:**345–46, **4E:117**
Brook Farm, **6E:195,** 195
Brooklyn Bridge, **11:**934; **12:**1038–39, **12E:432**
Brooks, Phillips, **11E:376**

Brooks, Preston, 7:558–59, *558–59*, **7E:228**

Browder, Earl, **13E:453**

Brown, Charles Brockden, **4E:117**

Brown, John, 7:557, *557*, **7E:228**, *229*

Brown, Moses, **5E:155–56**

Brown, Capt. Roy, **13:**1107

Browne, Carl, **10:***855*

Brownell, Kady, **8E:266**

Brownists, **1:**56

Brownson, Orestes, **6E:195**

Brown vs. Board of Education of Topeka, Kansas, **16:**1420; **17E:616**

Brown vs. Maryland (Original Package Case), 5:373, **5E:156**

Bruce, Blanche K., **10E:340**, *340*

Brulé, Etienne, **1E:5**

Brunel, Sir Marc Isambard, 5:447, **5E:156**

Bryan, William Jennings, 10:860, 886, *890*, **891–98**, *892–93, 895, 897*, **10E:340–41**; **12:**997, 1012

Bryan-Chammoro Treaty, **18E:657**

Bryant, William Cullen, **6E:195–96**

Buchanan, James, 6:528; 7:558, 588, 611, 612, 614, 616, **7E:229–30**, *229*

Buckner, Simon Bolivar, **8E:266**

Buell, Abel, **4E:117–18**

Buell, Gen. Don Carlos, 8:646, 647, **8E:266**

Buffalo, **9:**795–96

Buffalo Bill, *see* Cody, William F.

Buffalo soldiers, **9E:302**

Bull Run, First Battle of, **8:**636

Bull Run, Second Battle of, **8:**644

Bunau-Varilla, Philippe, 12:1026, **12E:411–12**, *412*

Bunche, Ralph Johnson, **16E:560–61**

Bunker Hill, Battle of, 3:187, *188–89*, 189, *191*, 211, 212, **3E:92**

Buntline, Ned, **9E:302–3**

Burbank, Luther, **13E:450**

Bureau of Indian Affairs, **9E:303**

Burger, Warren Earl, **17E:598–99**, *598*; **18:**1584

Burgoyne, John, 3:*216–18*, 219–20, **3E:80**, *80*

Burke, Edmund, **3E:80**, *80*

Burke, Edward R., **15:**1268

Burlington Railroad, **10:**850

Burnham, Daniel, **12E:412–13**, *412*

Burning Heart, **9:***782*

Burnside, Maj. Gen. Ambrose, 8:*646*, *647*, 847–48, **8E:266–67**, *267*

Burr, Aaron, 4:316, 337–38, **4E:118**, *118*

Burroughs, John, 13:*1164*, **13E:450–51**

Bush, George Herbert Walker, 1:7; 18:1552, 1569, **18E:637–38**, *637*

Busing, **17E:599**

Butler, Andrew Pickens, 7:558, **7E:230**

Butler, Benjamin F., **8E:267**; **10E:352**

Butler, John, **3E:81**

Butler, Pierce, 14:1254, **14E:487**

Butte, Montana, **9:**740

Butterfield, Alexander P., **17:**1483

Byrd, Harry F., **14E:488**

Byrd, Richard Evelyn, **14:**1210, *1210*, **14E:487–88**, *488*

Byrnes, James Francis, **3E:449**; **15E:523**

C

Cabeza de Vaca, Alvar Nuez, 1:39, *82*, **83–88**, *85* (map), **1E:5**

Cable, George Washington, 11:*968–69*, 970, **11E:376–77**

Cabot, John, 1:19, **1E:5–6**, *5*

Cabot, Sebastian, **1E:6**

Cabral, Pedro de, 1:19, **1E:6**

Cairo, **1:**17

Cairo Conference (1943), **15E:523–24**

Cajuns, **2E:40**

Calamity Jane, 9:739, **9E:303–4**, *303*

Caldwell, Erskine, 14:1222, **14E:488**

Calhoun, John C., **5:156–57**, *156*, 374, 391, 392; 6:520; 7:552, 553

    Eaton and, 5:394, 396, 406

    states' rights and, 5:398–99, *399*

    as vice president, 5:394

Calhoun, Mrs. John C., 5:394

California, **2E:41–42**; 6:455, 7:551–52; **10:**850

    acquisition of, 6:522–24

    gold in, **9:**20725, 730, 731, **734**

    gold rush in, 6:*469–85*, **6E:203–4**, 209

        California Argonauts, 6:524, **6E:196**

    Indians wars in, **9:**797–98

    Mexican War and, 7:*546*, *568–69*

Calley, William L., Jr., **17:**1447, 1449

Calvert, Cecilius, **2:**99

Calvert, Charles, **2E:46**, *46*

Calvert, George, 2:99, **2E:46**

Calvert, Leonard, 2:99, **2E:46**

Cambodia, **17:**1474, **17E:609–10**; **18:**1537

Camel Corps, **9E:304**

Cameron, Simon, **7E:230**

Camp David accords, **18:**1544–45

Canada, **6E:221**; **15:**1302, 1304

    American Revolution and, 3:209, *211*, 226

    colonial, **2:**154

    exploration of, **1E:6**, 7

    see also French and Indian War; New France; Quebec

Canals, 5:*420–21*, **432–35**, *432–34*, **5E:157**, *157*

Canarsee Indians, **1E:22**

Canby, Gen. E.R.S., **9E:304**

Canning, George, 5:369, **5E:157**

Cannon, Joseph Gurney, **12E:413**, *413*

Capitalism, **10:**823

    critics of, **10:**826

Capone, Alphonse ("Al"), 14:*1212*, 1212–13, **14E:488–89**

Capper-Volstead Cooperative Marketing Act (1922), **13**:1130

Caravels, **1E:6,** *6*

Caraway, Hattie, **14:***1214,* 1215, **14E:489**

Cardozo, Benjamin Nathan, **14:**1254, 1256, **14E:489–90,** *489*

Caribs, **1:***26,* **1E:**28

Carlisle, Lord Frederick Howard, **3:**222, **3E:81**

Carnegie, Andrew, **10:**816, 820, 825, *866–67,* 869, **10E:**349–50, 370; **11:**909, *960;* **12:***1070, 1071–78,* **12E:413**

Carnegie Steel Company, **10:**829–30, **10E:350**

Carolina Proprietors, **2E:46**

Carolinas, **2:**100–3
  see also North Carolina; South Carolina

Carpetbaggers, **8:**706, 707, *709,* 710

Carrington, Henry Beebee, **9:**792, **9E:304–5**

Cars, *see* Automobiles

Carson, Christopher (Kit), **6:**513–14, **6E:196,** *196;* **9:**797

Carson, Rachel Louis, **16E:561,** *561*

Carter, Clarence, **14:***1232*

Carter, Jimmy, **1:**7; **18:**1540–52, *1541, 1543, 1558,* **18E:**638–39, *639*
  civil rights under, **18:**1547–49
  election of 1976, **18:**1540–42
  election of 1980, **18:**1551–52
  energy crisis, **18:**1542
  the environment and, **18:**1549–50
  foreign policy and arms control, **18:**1544–47
  Iran crisis, **18:**1550–51
  refugee problems, **18:**1546–47

Carteret, Sir George, **2:**103, **2E:47**

Cartier, Jacques, **1E:6**

Carver, George Washington, **14E:490–91,** *490*

Carver, John, **1E:6–7**

Casablanca Conference (1943), **15:**1333, **15E:524,** *524*

Casa de Contratacin (House of Trade), **1:**40, 41

Casey, William Joseph, **18E:639–40**

Cass, Lewis, **7:**551, **7E:230**

Cassino, Monte, **15:**1301

Castro, Cipriano, **12:**1026, **12E:413–14**

Castro, Fidel, **16:**1418, *1418,* **16E:561**

Castro, Vaca de, *see* Vaca de Castro

Catholic Church (Catholics), **1E:5;** **10:887**
  in colonial America, **2E:46**
  Counter Reformation, **1E:8**
  election of 1960 and, **16:**1437
  in Middle Ages, **1:**14, 22
  in Spanish colonies, **1:**40, *41*

Catlin, George, **6E:196–97,** *197*

Cattle drives, **9:**744, *750–53,* **759–63,** *762–63*
  Indians and, **9:**755

Cattlemen, **9:759–68,** 775, **9E:**317; **10:**845
  Chisholm Trail and, **9E:305–6**
  kingdom of, **9:763–67**
  see also Cowboys

Catton, Bruce, **8:**713–18

Cavendish, Thomas, **1:***68–69* (map), *68–70,* **1E:7,** *7*

Central America, Reagan administration and, **18:**1568–69

Central Pacific Railroad, **9:**776, 806; **10:**821, *832–33,* 888, **10E:**360–61

Central Park (New York City), **11:***920,* **11E:394**

Cermak, Anton Joseph, **14:**1180, 1216, **14E:491**

Cervera, Adm. Pascual, **12:**1009, **12E:414**

Chaffee, Roger B., **17E:597**

Challenger space shuttle, **17:**1500, *1514,* 1517; **18:**1573–74, **18E:640**

Chamberlain, Neville, **14:**1226; **15:**1266, *1266,* **15E:524–25**

Chambers, Whittaker, **16:**1390

Champlain, Samuel de, **1:***33,* 43, **1E:7–8,** *8*

Chandler, Zachariah, **8E:267–68;** **11:**909

Chaplin, Charles Spencer (Charlie), **13E:451,** *451*

Chapman, John, **6E:197**

Chappel, Alonzo, **5E:157**

Chapultepec, battle of, **7:***576–77*

Charlesfort, **1E:30–31**

Charles I, King of England, **2:**96, 100, **2E:46, 47,** *47*

Charles I, King of Spain, **1:**41, **1E:5,** *8*

Charles II, King of England, **2:**100, 102–4, **2E:47**

Charles IV, King of Spain, **4E:118,** *118*

Charleston (South Carolina), **2:**101
  American Revolution and, **3:**210–11, *212–13,* 222
  Battle of, **3E:100, 101**
  colonial, **2:***140*

Charles V, Holy Roman Emperor, *see* Charles I, King of Spain

Chase, Salmon P., **7E:230–31**

Chavez, Cesar Estrada, **17E:599,** *599*

Cherokees, **5:**397, **5E:157–58,** 185

Chesapeake, **4:***326, 327,* 340

Cheves, Langdon, **6E:197**

Cheyenne Indians, **9:**792, 794, *794,* 796, **9E:**301, 302, 304, 307, 308, 310, 316–17, 325

Chiang Kai-shek, **15:**1333–34, **15E:525**

Chicago, **12E:412–13**
  fire (1871), **9E:305,** *305*
  1968 riots, **17:**1456, 1458

Chicago, Burlington & Quincy Railroad, **9:**776, 805–7; **10:**872

Chicago, Milwaukee & St. Paul Railroad, **9:**776

Chicago Seven, the, **17E:599–600**

Chickamauga, Battle of, **8:**672–73, *673*

Child labor, **5:**427–28; **12:**1055, *1056–57*

Children, **12:**1055
  see also Education

Chile, **1E:3**

China, **12:**1029, 1035, **12E:**438; **13:**1102, 1134; **15:**1265, **15E:525**
  Boxer Rebellion, **12:***1030–31,* 1032, **12E:411**
  Korean War and, **16:**1387, 1388
  Nixon and, **17:1478**

China (*cont.*)
  open-door policy toward, **12:***1028–29,* 1032
  present-day, **18:***1553–59*
  World War II and, **15:**1274
Chinese Exclusion Act, **10E:341**
Chinese immigrants, **10:**833, 834, 888, **10E:**341
Chinese Revolution, **15E:**525; **16:**1385–86
Chisholm, Jesse, **9E:**306
Chisholm Trail, **9E:305–6**
Chisholm vs. Georgia, **18:**1594
Chivington, Col. J. M., **9:**781, *781*
Chivington, John Milton, **9E:306**
Chou En-lai, **17:**1478
Christian Science, **9E:**310
  see also Eddy, Mary Baker
Christian Socialism, **10E:**364; **11E:**399
Churches, *see* Religion; *specific denominations*
Churchill, Sir Winston, **15:**1271, *1272,* 1296, 1311,
  15E:526; **16:**1356
Church of England, **1:**49, 56, 58, 68, **1E:8**
Church of Jesus Christ of Latter-Day Saints, *see*
  Mormons
Cibola, Seven Cities of, **1:**39, **1E:8–9**
Cincinnati, Society of the, **3E:81**
CIO, *see* Committee for Industrial Organization
Circus, **11:**940
  see also Barnum, Phineas T.
Cisneros, Evangelina, **12:**1002–3
Cities
  bosses and political machines, **11:913–14**
  of Europe (15th-16th century), **1:**12, 14
  growth of (late 19th-early 20th century),
    12:1049–50
  late 19th century, **11:931–46**
  modernization of, **12:***1037–47*
  reform movement and, **11:943–46**
  slums, late 19th century, **11:**943, *944–45,* 945,
    11E:396
  see also specific cities
Civilian Conservation Corps, **14:**1183
Civil rights, **9E:**300; **16E:**571, 573
  in 1950s and 1960s, **16:1420–24**
  in 1970s, **18:1538–39, 1547–49**
  Carter administration and, **18:**1547–49
  gay rights, **18:***1552*
  reverse discrimination, **18:**1549
  Supreme Court cases
    Brown vs. Board of Education of Topeka,
      Kansas, **16:**1420, **16E:**561; **17E:**616
    Plessy vs. Ferguson, **10E:363**
  see also Blacks; Civil Rights Act; Civil rights
    movement; Segregation; Slavery
Civil Rights Act
  of 1866, **8:**702, 703, **8E:268**
  of 1957, **16:**1421, **16E:**562
  of 1960, **16E:**562
  of 1964, **16:**1426, **16E:**562

Civil-rights movement, **16:1420–24, 16E:561–62**;
  17E:600–1, 613–14
  in Birmingham, **16:**1422, **16E:**562
  CORE (Congress of Racial Equality), **16E:**562
  freedom rides, **16:**1421, **16E:**562
  March on Washington (1963), **16:**1423, *1423,*
    16E:562
  Montgomery bus boycott, **16E:**562
  NAACP (National Association for the Advance-
    ment of Colored People), **15E:**527, 528;
    17E:600
  SCLC (Southern Christian Leadership Confer-
    ence), **18E:**654
  Selma march (1965), **16:***1422*
  SNCC (Student Non-Violent Coordinating Com-
    mittee), **17E:**598
  see also individual civil rights leaders
Civil Service Commission, **10:**878, **10E:**362
Civil War, U.S., **3:**248; **7:**547; **8:635–54, 667–84,**
  8E:262–96; **9:**769, **9E:**300, 318; **10:**887
  Alabama claims and, **9E:**299
  armies, **8:***712–17,* **713–18**
    Confederate, **8:**635
    Union, **8:**635–37, 671
  casualties, **8:**638, 646, 648, 677, 684, 718
  Davis and, **8:**635
  economy and, **8:**667–69, 698
  effects of, **10:**815
  Europe and, **8:**647
  Grant's strategy, **8:673, 676–81**
  industrialization and, **5:443–48**; **8:**698, **8E:**271;
    10:818
  Lee's strategy, **8:642–45**
  Lincoln and, **8:**635, 642, 645, 647, 648, 654, 655,
    655–62, 679–80
  mining and, **9:**726
  naval war, **8:**685, *685–96*
  Northern victories, **8:**637–39, 649–51, 673,
    676–84
  origins of, **5:**398
  prisons and, **8:**670, *670,* **8E:**262
  Radical Republicans and, **8:**644–45, 710
  recruitment for, **8:***669,* 669–70
  sectionalism prior to, **5:**398; **7:549–60**
  slavery and, **8:**671, 718
  start of, **7:**618–19
  weapons used, **8:**718
  the West and, **9:**725, 726
  women in, **8E:**266, 269, 275, 280
  see also Reconstruction
Clanton, Ike, **10E:**347
Clark, Champ, **13:**1091, **13E:451–52**
Clark, George Rogers, **4E:**119, *119*
Clark, Gen. Mark Wayne, **15:**1297–98, **15E:526–27,**
  527
Clark, Capt. William, **4:**336; **6:**511–12, *512–13*
  see also Lewis and Clark expedition

Clay, Henry, **4**:344–45; **5**:367, 391, 392, *395,*
    5E:158; **6**:492, 520; **7**:*552,* 552–53
  national bank and, **5**:401–2
Clay, Gen. Lucius D., **16E:559**
Clay Compromise Tariff, *see* Compromise of 1833
Clayton Antitrust Act of 1914, **12**:1053, **12E:414**
Clayton-Bulwer Treaty, **6E:197–98**; **12**:1025
Clemenceau, Georges, **13**:1093, 1100, 1101, 1102,
    1103, **13E:452,** *452*
Clemens, Samuel, *see* Twain, Mark
Clement VII, Pope, **1E:17**
Cleveland, Grover, **10**:830, 856–60, *878,* 879, 880,
    881, 885, 893–94, **10E:341–42,** *342*; **11:***910,*
    913; **12**:996, 998; **14:***1191*
Clinton, DeWitt, **5**:433, 437, **5E:159,** *159*
Clinton, George, **4**:338, **4E:119**
Clinton, Sir Henry, **3**:210; **3E:81**
Clipper ships, **7**:589, *600–7*
Clothes (fashion), late 19th century, **11**:908–9, *908,*
    954–55, 976–77
Clyfton, Richard, **1**:54, **1E:9**; **2**:171, 173
Clyman, James, **6E:198**
Cobb, Howell, **7E:231,** *231*
Cochise, **9**:797, **9E:306**
Cochrane, Elizabeth, **11**:939, **11E:377,** *377*
Cody, William F. (Buffalo Bill), **9E:303**; **11**:940,
    940–41, **11E:377–78,** *377*
Cohan, George M., **13**:1099, **13E:452**
Cohen, Benjamin, **14E:486**
Cohens vs. Virginia, **5E:159**; **18**:1598
Colbert, Jean Baptiste, **1**:44, **1E:9**
Cold War, **16:1385–94,** 1418, 1434–36
Colfax, Schuyler, **8E:268**
Colleges and universities, **11**:942–43, 961; **12**:1069
  see also Education
Collins, Michael, **17:***1479, 1494, 1495,* **17E:597**
Colombia, **12**:1026
Colonial America, **2:95–137,** *137–49*
  blacks in, **2:***146,* **2E:42**
  Confederation of New England, **2**:98–99
  democracy in, **2E:74**
  disunity in, **3**:189, 195, 196, 245, 254
  economy, **2:***144, 145, 147–49*
  England and, **2:95–108, 124–36**
  France and, **2**:99, 105, **125–36**
  French and Indian War and, **2:134–36,** 109,
    109–22, **2E:52,** *52*
  freedom of the press in, **2E:74**
  Fundamental Constitutions of Carolina, **2**:100–1
  Fundamental Orders of Connecticut, **2**:97
  government of, **2**:97–99, 100, **104–8**
  growth of, **2:96–100**
  Holland and, **2**:99, 100, 102
  Indians in, **2**:97, 98, 125, 128–30, *146,* **2E:67**
  Massachusetts, **1**:77; **2**:95–96
  Massachusetts Bay Company and, **2:96–99,** 171,
    173

Colonial America (*cont.*)
  piedmonters, **2**:123
  population of, **2**:95–96
  Quakers, **2**:103–5
  religious issues in, **2:95–99, 2E:46**
  Roman Catholics in, **2E:46**
  social issues in, **2**:100–2, 108, 123–24, *146*
  smuggling in, **2**:155
  Spain and, **2**:100, 105–6, 124–25, 127–28, 130–31
  trade in, **2**:95, 102
  the West and, **2**:97, 105, 123–26
  see also American Revolution; Dutch colonies;
    French and Indian War; French colonies;
    Spanish colonies; *and specific American*
    colonies
Colorado, **9**:725, 730
  gold in, **9**:732–33
Colt, Samuel, **5:***447,* **5E:159**; **10**:818
Columbus, Christopher, **1:***10,* **11–12, 18–20,** 22, 23,
    39–40, **1E:9–10,** 3
Comanches, **9**:796–97
Committee for Industrial Organization (later the
    Congress of Industrial Organizations;
    C.I.O.), **13E:461**; **14**:1223–24, **14E:500**
Committees of Correspondence, **2E:47–48**
Common Sense (Paine), **3**:189, *199,* **3E:81–82**
Communications
  in early 20th century, **12:1062–64**
  Atlantic cable, **11E:381–82**
  telegraph, **5E:160,** 174; **9**:795; **10**:825, **10E:348**;
    11:*935,* **11E:381–82**
  telephone, **10**:818, *822,* 825, **10E:338**; **11**:936;
    12:1062–64, *1065*
  see also Radio; Television
Communist Party and communists, American
  blacklisting of Hollywood Ten, **16E:569–70,** *569*
  McCarthy and McCarthyism, **16**:1390–92,
    16E:576–77
  Red Scare (1920s), **13**:1155–56, **13E:452–53,** *453*
  Rosenberg spy case, **16E:584–85,** *584*
Comogre, Cacique, **1E:4**
Compromise of 1833, **5E:159**
Compromise of 1850, **7:***552,* 552–54, 626–28,
    7E:231–32
Compton, Arthur H., **14E:500**
Computers, **17:1503–10**
Comstock, Henry, **9E:306**
Comstock Lode, **9**:731, *733,* **9E:306–7**
Concord, Battle of, **3**:185–86, 189, **3E:84, 88,** 91
Conestoga wagon, **5**:431–32, **5E:159–60**
Confederate States of America, **7**:615–16, **7E:232,**
    232
  see also Civil War, U.S.
Confederation of New England, **2**:98–99
Congregationalists, **2**:171–73; **3**:250
  see also Half-way Covenant
Congress, Continental, *see* Continental Congress

Congress, U.S., **10:**880, 881, 884, 885, *882–83,* 887
Constitutional Convention and, **4E:**286–88
  industrial regulation and, **10:**826
  Western lands and, **9:773–95**
  see also Continental Congress
Congress of Racial Equality (C.O.R.E.),
    16E:562
Congress of the Confederation, **3E:**82
  see also Continental Congress
Conkling, Roscoe, **10:**877, **10E:342–43**; **11:**912
Connecticut, colonial, **2:**97, 98
Connecticut Blue Laws, **2E:**49, 50
Connecticut Charter of 1662, **2E:48**
Connecticut Compromise, **4E:119**
Connor, Eugene "Bull," **16:**1422
Connor, Gen. Patrick Edward, **9:**792, **9E:307**
Conquistadors, Spanish, **1:**22, 23, *29–33,* 37–39,
    1E:27
Conservation movement, **9E:**319
Constantinople, **1:**14, 17
Constitution, U.S., **2E:**54; **3E:**79, 83, 96, 98, 111;
    4E:120; **18:**1576, **1589–98**
  Bicentennial of, **18:**1577, *1582–87*
  Connecticut Compromise, **4E:119**
  The Federalist and, **4:**290
  influences on, **2E:**56
  interpretation of, **4:**307; **5:**371–72
  New Jersey Plan, **4:**285, 286, **4E:137–38**
  ratification of, **4:**289–90
  separation of powers and, **4:**288
  Supreme Court and, **5E:**172
  taxation and, **4:**286–87
  Virginia Plan, **4:***284,* 286, **4E:146**
  see also Bill of Rights; Constitutional Conven-
    tion; Supreme Court, U.S.; *and specific*
    amendments (*e.g.* Fourteenth Amendment)
Constitution ("Old Ironsides"), **4:***319–21, 324–25,*
    4E:119–20
Constitutional Convention, **3E:**79; **4:***282–83,*
    284–90, *287, 288*
Constitutional Union Party, **7:**609
Constitutions, state, **3:**245–48
Consumer movement, **17E:**620–21
Contadora peace plan, **18:**1569
Continental Army, **3:**186, 187, 189, 196, 213, 217,
    227, *228, 230–37, 240, 242–43, 258–59,* 264,
    265, 267, **3E:**82, 90, **91,** 94, 109
  Minutemen and, **3E:**98
  see also American Revolution
Continental Association, **3:**185, **3E:**82
Continental Congress, **3:***204,* 253, 254, **3E:82–83**
  Articles of Confederation and, **3:***255–56*
  First, **3:**185, 251–52, **3E:**82
  Second, **3E:**79, 82, **83,** 91, 92, 186
  weakness of, **4:**278–82
Continental Navy, **3E:**91
Contras, **18:**1546, 1569, **18E:**658
  Iran-Contra affair, **18E:650–53**

Convention of 1800 (Treaty of Morfontaine), **4:**316,
    4E:120
Convention of 1818, **5:**365–66, **5E:160**
Conway, Thomas, **3E:83**
Conwell, Russell H., **11:**962–63, **11E:378**
Cooke, Jay, **8:**667–68, **8E:268,** *268*; **10E:**361;
    11:907–8
Coolidge, Calvin, **10:**891; **13:**1120, *1120,* **1124–26,**
    1125, 1134, **13E:453–54**
Cooper, James Fenimore, **6:**495, **6E:198**
Cooper, L. Gordon, Jr., **17:***1491*
Cooper, Peter, **5:**377, *386–87,* **5E:160,** *160*; **10E:**352
Copley, John Singleton, **3E:83,** *83*
Copperheads, *see* Wood, Fernando
Coral Sea, Battle of the, **15:***1292–93,* 1293
Corbin, Abel, **10:**865
Corbin, Margaret Cochrane, *see* Molly Pitcher
Corcoran, Thomas G., **14E:**486
CORE (Congress of Racial Equality), **16E:**562
Cornwallis, Lord Charles, **3:**210, 213, 223, 264,
    266–68, **3E:83–84**
Coronado, Francisco Vasquez, **1:**39, **1E:**3, 10
Corporations, Fourteenth Amendment and,
    10:826–27
Corruption, political, **10:**821–22, 875–77
  bosses and political machines, **11:913–14**
  Credit Mobilier scandal, **10:**821–22, **10E:343**
  Peralta land fraud, **9E:**321–22, *321* (map)
  Teapot Dome scandal, **13:**1123, 1124, 1133–34,
    13E:475, 478
Cortez, Hernando, **1:***29–31,* 37, **1E:**4, **10–11,** *10*
Cosa, Juan de la, **1:**24, **1E:11**
Cotton, **7:582–86**; **8:**698
Cotton, John, **2:**174, *176,* **2E:48**
Cotton gin, **5:***378,* 442, **443–46,** *445*; **7:**582–83
Cotton Kingdom, **5E:160–61,** *161*
Council of the Indies, **1:**41–43
Council of Trent, **1E:8**
Counter Reformation, **1E:8**
Cowan, John, **9:**737
Cowboys, **9:***741–58*; **10:**845, *847*
  black, **9E:**322–23
  as heros, **9:**767–68
  roundup, **9:***744–45*
  in town, **9:***756–57*
  on the trail, **9:***740–41*
  vaquero, **9:***742–43*
  work of, **9:***748–49*
Cow towns, **9:***754–55, 760–63, 766–67*
Cox, Archibald, **17:**1481, 1483
Cox, James Middleton, **13:**1121, **13E:454**
Coxey, Jacob Sechler, **10:***855,* 858, **10E:343,** *343*
Crane, Stephen, **11:**967, **11E:378–79,** *378*
Crawford, William, **5:**391, 392, **5E:161**; **6:**492
Crazy Horse, **9:**792, 796, **9E:307**
Credit Mobilier scandal, **10:**821–22, **10E:343**
Cree Indians, **9E:**302
Creek Indians, **2E:**62; **4E:**128

Creel, George, **13**:1094–95, 1098, **13E:454–55**
Crick, Francis H. C., **17**:1512
Crime
  Great Diamond Fraud, **9E:313**
  smuggling, in colonial America, **2**:155
  see also Corruption, political; Outlaws
Crittenden, John Jordan, **7**:*614, 615*, **7E:232–33**
Crittenden Compromise, **7E:233**
Crockett, David ("Davy"), **7**:*562*, **7E:233**, *233*
Croker, Richard, **11**:*912*
Cromwell, Oliver, **2**:100, **2E:48**, *48*
Crook, Gen. George, **9**:796, **9E:304**
"Cross of Gold" speech, **10**:860, 894, **10E:341**
Crow Indians, **9**:735
Crown Point, Battle of, **2**:*116*
Crusades, **1**:14, *16,* 18
Cuba, **1**:11; **16**:1418, **16E:561**
  19th-century, **12**:**997–1009**, *999*
  Bay of Pigs invasion, **16**:1434, **16E:5**
  Ostend Manifesto, **7E:247**
  refugees from, **18**:1546–47, *1547*
  Spanish-American War and, **12**:1006–9, *1007,
    1013–23*
Cuban missile crisis (1962), **16**:1418–19
Cumberland Road, **5**:430–31, **5E:161**
Cummings, Homer Stille, **14**:1254, **14E:491**
Currency Act (1764), **2**:155
Currier and Ives lithographs, **11**:*919–29*, **11E:379**
Curry, John Steuart, **14**:1227, *1230*
Curtis, Charles, **13**:1126, **13E:455**
Curtis, George William, **10**:876
Curtiss, Glenn, **12**:1060, **12E:414**, *414*
Cushman, Pauline, **8E:269**
Custer, George Armstrong, **9**:739, *785–87,* 796,
  9E:307–8, *308*, 308–9
Custer's Last Stand, **9E:308–9**, *308*
Cut Nose, **9**:*778,* 779, **9E:309**
Cuyler, Theodore, **11E:379**
Cuzco, **1E:3**
Cyclotron, **14**:1215, **14E:450, 499**
Czechoslovakia, **14**:1226; **15**:1266

D

Da Gama, Vasco, **1**:18, **1E:11**, *11*
Dahlgren, John Adolphus, **8E:269**
Dana, Charles Anderson, **11**:938, **11E:379–80**,
  379
Dana, Richard Henry, **5E:161–62**
Dances, **10**:*814*
Dare, Virginia, **1E:11**
Darien, **1E:11**, 4
Darrow, Clarence Seward, **10**:897, *897*, **10E:344**,
  344
Dartmouth College case, **7**:624
Darwin, Charles, **11**:959

Darwinism, **11**:914
  Social, **11**:960–61, **11E:382**
Daugherty, Harry M., **13**:1119, *1120*, 1121, 1123,
  1124, **13E:455**, 461
Davenport, John, **2E:49**
Davila, Pedrarias, **1E:5**
Davis, James John, **13E:455**
Davis, Jefferson, **5E:162**; **7**:556, *617,* **7E:233–34**,
  234; **8**:635, *637,* 642, 680, **8E:269–670**;
  9E:304
Davis, John, **1E:11–12**
Davis, John William, **13**:1124, **13E:455–56**
Davis, Richard Harding, **12**:999, **12E:415**, *415*
Davis, Stuart, **14**:*1235*
Davison, Sir William, **1**:*49*
Dawes, William, **3**:185, **3E:84**, *84*
Dawes Severalty Act, **9E:309**
Day, Stephen, **2E:49**
Dayton, Jonathan, **4E:120–21**, *120*
D-Day, **15**:*1275–89, 1280–81* (map)
Deadwood, South Dakota, **9**:*738,* 739
Dean, John, **17**:1481, **17E:628**
Deane, Silas, **2E:84**, *84*
Dearborn, Henry, **4E:121**
Death penalty, **3**:252
Debs, Eugene, **10**:*827,* 830
Debs, Eugene Victor, **10E:344–45**, *345*
Decatur, Capt. Steven, **4**:*322*, **4E:121**
Declaration of Independence, **3**:190–93, *197–208,*
  254, **3E:85**, *85*
Deerfield Massacre, *see* Queen Anne's War
Deficit, federal budget, **17**:1477; **18**:1563–64
De Forest, Lee, **12**:1062, **12E:415**
De Gaulle, Charles, **15**:1304
De Grasse, Count François Joseph Paul, **3E:85–86**
Dehn, Adolf, **14**:*1241*
De Kooning, Willem, **16**:*1368*
Delaware, colonial, **1E:26**; **2**:104
Delaware, Lackawanna & Western Railroad,
  10:828
De Lome Letter, *see* Dupuy de Lome, Enrique
De Long, George Washington, **9E:314**
Democracy, **1**:8
  in colonial America, **2E:74**
  property laws and, **3**:250
Democratic Party, **5**:401; **7**:557, 558, 560; **10**:856,
  857, 858–60, 878–80, 885, 891, 893, 897–98
  Reconstruction and, **8**:708–9
  slavery and, **7**:588, 609
  see also Elections
Democratic-Republican Party, **4**:314, 316, 349;
  5:730
  Jefferson and, **4**:333
Dempsey, William Harrison (Jack), **13**:1150, *1150,*
  13E:456, *456*, 476
Denby, Edwin, **13**:1123
Dennis et al. vs. United States, **14E:484–85**
Denver, **9**:732–33, 740

Denver & Rio Grande Railway, **9:**776
Den Xiaoping, **18:***1558*
Depression
  of 1870s-1890s, **10E:361–62**
  of 1893, **10:**856–57
  of 1930s, *see* Great Depression
Deregulation of industry, **18E:641,** *641*
Desert Land Act of 1877, **9:**774, **9E:309–10; 10:**845
De Soto, Hernando, **1:**38, **1E:12,** *12*
Detente, **18:**1539
Deuterium, **14:**1212
Dew, Thomas Roderick, **7:**587
Dewey, Commodore George, **12:***994, 1003,* 1006,
  1009, 1012, **12E:415–16**
Dewey, John, **11E:380; 12:**1066, 1069
Dewey, Thomas Edmund, **16:**1364, **16E:562–63,**
  563
Diaz, Bartholomew, **1:**18, **1E:12–13,** *12*
Diaz, Porfirio, **12E:416**
Dickinson, Emily, **11E:380,** *380*
Dickinson, John, **2:**164; **3:**194, **3E:86**
Diem, Ngo Dinh, **17:**1445
Dien Bien Phu, **17:**1445
Diet of Worms, **1E:8**
Dillinger, John, **14:**1213
Dime novels, **9E:302–3**
Dine, Jim, **16:***1378*
Dingley Tariff, **10:**880, **10E:345**
Dinwiddie, Robert, **2:**132, **2E:49**
Dirksen, Everett McKinley, **16E:563–64,** *563*
Disarmament, *see* Arms control and disarmament
Disney, Walt, **14:**1209, *1211,* **14E:491–92,** *492*
Dissent, **4:**290
Distribution-Preemption Act of 1841, **6:**456,
  6E:198; 10:845
Distribution system, industry and, **10:**825–26
District of Colombia, **4E:**146
  see also Washington, D.C.
Dix, Dorothea Lynde, **6E:199**
Dixiecrats, **16:**1364
DNA, **17:**1512–13
Dodge City, Kansas, **9:***755,* 761
Doheney, Edward L., **13:**1123, **13E:475**
Dole, Elizabeth, **18E:641–42,** *642*
Dole, Robert Joseph, **18E:642–43,** *643*
Dollar diplomacy, **12:**1033–35, **12E:424**
Dominican Republic, **12:**1027–28
Doniphan, Alexander William, **7:**549, **7E:234–35**
Donnelly, Ignatius, **10:**856, **10E:345,**
Donner Party, **7E:235,** *235*
Doolittle, James H., **15:**1293, **15E:527**
Dos Passos, John, **13:**1160, *1161,* **13E:456–57,** *457*
Doubleday, Abner, **11E:381**
Douglas, Stephen A., **7:**555, 588, 609–11,
  7E:236–37, *236*
Douglas, William Orvill, **16E:564**
Douglass, Frederick, **7E:235–36**

Draft, military, **17E:601–2,** *601*
  Civil War and, **8:**669
Draft riots, **8E:270–71,** *270*
Drago Doctrine, **12E:416**
Drake, "Colonel" E. L., **10:**816, *817,* **10E:345–46**
Drake, Sir Francis, **1:**63, *70,* 70, 72, **1E:13,** *13*
Dred Scott case, **5:***422;* **7:**559–60, **7E:237**
Dreiser, Theodore, **13E:457**
Dresser, Paul, **12E:416**
Drew, Daniel, **10:**862, **10E:346, 11:**905
Du Bois, William Edward Burghardt, **15E:527–28,**
  527
Dudingston, William, **2:**165, 166
Dudley, Joseph, **2E:49–50,** *49*
Dudley, Thomas, **2:**174, **2E:50**
Due process, **10:**827
Duke, James Buchanan, **10E:346**
Dulles, John Foster, **16:**1394, **16E:564–65**
Dull Knife, **9E:310**
Dunbar, William, **6:**512, **6E:199**
Dunkirk, **15:**1268, *1269*
Dunne, Finley Peter, **12E:416**
Du Pont, Eleuther Irenee, **5E:162**
Dupuy de Lome, Enrique, **12:**997, 1003–4,
  12E:416–17
Durer, Albrecht, **1:**34
Duryea brothers, **12E:417,** *417*
Dust storms (1934), **14:***1219,* 1219–20
Dutch colonies, **1:**47–48, 64; **1E:***25;* **2:**99, 100, 102,
  103
Dutch explorers and settlers, **1:**47–48
Dutch West India Company, **1:**47, 48, **1E:13**
Dylan, Bob, **17E:602,** *602*

E

Eads, James Buchanan, **8E:271,** *271*
Eagleton, Thomas, **17:**1480
Eakins, Thomas, **11:***972,* 973; **12E:417**
Eames, Emma, **12E:417**
Earhart, Amelia, **14:***1214,* 1225, **14E:492**
Early, Jubal Anderson, **8:***680,* 681, **8E:271–72**
Earp, Wyatt, **10E:346–47,** *346*
Eastern Europe, after World War II, **16:**1356–57
East Germany, **16:**1356, 1418
East India Company, **1:**67
East Indies, **1:**20
Eastman, Seth, **6E:199**
Eastman Kodak Company, **10E:347**
Eastman, George, **10E:347,** *347*
Eaton, John Henry, **5:**394, 406, **5E:162**
Eaton, Peggy O'Neale Timberlake, **5:**394, *405,*
  5E:162–63, *162*
Eaton, Theophilus, **2E:50**
Eaton, William, **4E:121**

Eckert, J. Presper, Jr., **17**:1505
Ecology, *see* Environment, the
Economy, the
  19th century
    Civil War, **8**:667–69, 698
    immigration and, **10:886–89**
    politics and, **10:875–89**
    tariffs, **10:879–80,** *881–83*
    see also Gilded Age
  in 1960s, **16**:1415–16
  in 1970s, **18**:1537, 1542
  in 1980s, **18:1562–64**
  post-revolutionary, **4**:276, 282, 283
  under Washington, **4:304–8**
  after World War II, **16**:1355–56
  see also Capitalism; Depression; Industrializa-
    tion; Industry; Panic; Tariffs; Taxation;
    Trade; *and other specific topics*
Eddy, Mary Baker, **9E:310**
Eddy, Thomas, **6E:199**
Edgar, Henry, **9**:736
Edict of Nantes, **1E:17**
Edison, Thomas Alva, **10**:818, 820, 821, *823,*
    10E:347–48, *347*; **11**:935; **13:***1164,*
    13E:465
Education, **4**:285
  19th century, **5E:171–72**; **6**:465, 494–95,
    6E:191–92; **11:941–43**
  early 20th century, **12**:1066, 1069
  of blacks, **11E:404**
    Brown vs. Board of Education of Topeka,
    Kansas, **16**:1420; **17E:616**
  colleges and universities, **11**:942–43, 961;
    12:1069
  G.I. Bill of Rights, **16E:568**
  right to, **3**:252
  segregation of schools, *see* Segregation
  of women, **11**:942
  after World War II, **16**:1358
Edward VI, King of England, **1E:8**
Edward VIII, King of England, **14:***1223,* 1225
Edwards, Jonathan, **2E:50,** *50,* 53
Egypt, **16**:1393; **17**:1451; **18**:1539, 1544–45
Ehrlichman, John, **17**:1481
Eighteen-Nation Disarmament Committee
    (ENDC), **16E:580**
Eighteenth Amendment, **12**:1056, **12E:417–18,** *418*;
    13:1151–52
Einstein, Albert, **14**:1218; **15**:1310, **15E:528–29,** *528*
Einstein, Isadore, **13E:465**
Eisenhower, Dwight D., **1**:6; **9E:32**; **15:***1301*;
    16:1389–99, 1420, **16E:565–66,** *565*; **17**:1445
  election of 1952, **16**:1389
  in World War II, **15**:1276, 1296, **15E:529–30**
Eisenhower Doctrine, **16E:565**
Elections
  1800, **4**:316

Elections (*cont.*)
  1804, **4**:338
  1808, **4**:338
  1824, **5**:392
  1828, **5**:392, 393
  1832, **5**:402, 406
  1844, **6**:520–21
  1848, **7**:551–52
  1852, **7**:554
  1856, **7**:557–58
  1858, **7**:560
  1860, **7:609–12**
  1876, **8**:708–9, **8E:264**; **10**:877
  1880, **10E:350**
  1888, **10**:880
  1892, **10**:855–56, 893
  1894, **10**:856, 894
  1896, **10:***857,* **858–60,** 894, *895,* 896–97
  1900, **10**:897
  1904, **10**:897
  1908, **10**:897
  1912, **10**:897
  1920, **13**:1119–21
  1928, **13**:1126
  1934, **14**:1242–43
  1936, **14**:1244–45
  1938, **14**:1248–49
  1946, **16**:1359
  1948, **16**:1362, *1363,* 1364
  1956, **16**:1394
  1960, **16**:1416
  1964, **16**:1426–27
  1968, **17**:1454, 1458
  1972, **17:1478–80**
  1976, **18:1540–42**
  1980, **18**:1551–52
  1984, **18**:1569–70
Electoral College, **4**:287–88, **4E:121–22**
Electoral process, **4**:287–88, 338
Electricity (electric power), **10E:368**; **11**:932;
    12:*1040–41,* **1060,** 1062
Electric light, **10**:818, 820, 821, **10E**:348; **12**:1060,
    1064; **13**:1128–29
Eleventh Amendment, **18**:1597
Eliot, John, **2:***94,* **2E:50–51**
Elizabeth I, Queen of England, **1:***49,* 70, *71,* 71,
    1E:13
Ellis Island, **10E:348–49,** *348*
Ellsberg, Daniel, **17E:622–24**
Ellsworth, Oliver, **4E:122**
Ellwood, Isaac, **9**:770
El Salvador, **18**:1568
Ely, Joseph B., **14**:1244, **14E:492–93**
Ely, Richard Theodore, **11E:381**
Emancipation Proclamation, **8:***660,* **8E:271–72**
Embargo Act, **4**:340–41, *342–43,* **4E:122**
Embree, Elihu, **6E:199**

Emergency Banking Act (1933), **14:**1182–83
Emergency Committee for Unemployment Relief, **14:**1177–78
Emergency Farm Mortgage Act, **14:**1185
Emerson, Ralph Waldo, **6:**491, 495, **6E:199–200,** *200, 219*
Emmett, Daniel Decatur, **7E:237**
Empire State Building, **14E:493,** *493*
Encomienda, **1E:30**
Endecott, John, **1E:29; 2:**95–96, *96,* **2E:51,** *51*
Energy crisis, **17E:602–3**
Engel vs. Vitale, **14E:485**
England, *see* Great Britain
ENIAC computer, **17:**1505
Entertainment, **16:***1395–1413*
    late 19th century, **11:939–41**
    in 1920s, **13:**1148–49, 1158
    in 1930s, **14:**1221–23
    see also specific forms of entertainment (e.g.,
        Movies; Television; Theater)
Environment, the, **18:**1549–50
    conservation movement, **9E:319**
Environmental Protection Agency (EPA), **17:**1477,
    17E:603–4
EPIC (End Poverty In California), **14:**1220
Equality, **6:**496
Equal Rights Amendment, **18:**1538–39, **18E:643**
Era of Good Feelings, **5:**370, 376, 391
Erdman Act, **10E:364**
Ericsson, John, **8E:272,** *272, 688, 691*
Eric the Red, **1E:13–14**
Erie, Lake, **1E:5**
Erie Canal, **5:***420, 421,* **5E:163**
Erie Railroad, **10:**862, **10E:346,** 349, 352
Erikson, Leif, **1E:14**
Erlichman, John, **17E:628–29**
Ervin, Sam J., **17:**1481, **17E:628**
Estaing, Count Charles Hector, **3E:86**
Ethiopia, **15:**1265
European Recovery Program, *see* Marshall Plan
Evans, Oliver, **5:***382, 383,* **5E:163**
Everett, Edward, **7E:237**
Evers, Charles, **17E:600**
Evers, Medgar, **16:**1422–23
Everson vs. Board of Education, **14E:484**
Evolution, **11:**914, 959
    Scopes trial and, **10:***897,* 898, **10E:366**
Ewell, Richard, **8:**654, **8E:272–73**
Ewing, Thomas, **5E:163**
Executive branch, **4:**288
    see also President, the
Explorations and discoveries
    15th-16th century, **1:17–22,** **37–39,** **1E:6,** 21–22,
        24 (map), 35–36, *37* (map)
        Cabeza de Vaca, **1:83–88,** *85* (map)
    the West, **6:531–38**
    see also individual explorers and discoverers

Factory system, **5:**425–28
Fairfax, Thomas, **3E:86**
Fair Labor Standards Act of 1938, **14:**1247
Fairweather, Bill, **9:**736
Fall, Albert B., **13:***1120,* 1123
Fall, Andrew B., **13:**1121
Fallen Timbers, Battle of, **4E:122–23,** *122*
Familists, **1:**56
Farley, James Aloysius, **14E:493**
Farm Credit Administration, **15E:539**
Farmers
    Granges and, **10E:352,** 356
    National Farmers' Alliance, **10E:359–60**
    see also Agriculture
Farm failures, **18E:643–44**
Farming, *see* Agriculture
Farragut, David Glasgow, **8E:273,** *273*
Farrell, James Thomas, **14:**1222, **14E:493–94,** *494*
Fast Mail, **10:***831*
Faubus, Orval E., **16:**1420
Faulkner, William, **14:**1222; **16E:566–67,** *566*
Federal Arts Project, **14:**1221, *1242*
Federal Emergency Relief Administration,
    14:1183, 1185
Federal Farm Board, **13:**1130–31
Federal government, **4:**309
    American Revolution and, **3:**245–54, 256–57
    Articles of Confederation and, **3:**254–57; **4:**275
    in colonial America, **2:**100, **104–8**
    industry and, **10:**824, 825
    Northwest Ordinance and, **4:**285
    post-revolutionary, **3:**245–54, 256–57; **4:**276–85
        Congress and, **4:**278–82
        disunity in, **4:**278–83
    separation of church and state, **2:**98
    states' rights and, **4:**315–16; **5:**398–400, *399*
    Supreme Court and, **5:**370–74
    see also Congress, U.S.; Constitution, U.S.;
        President, the
Federal Housing Act of 1949, **16:**1420
Federal Immigration Act (1891), **10:***888,* **10E:349**
Federal Intermediate Credit Act of 1923, **13:**1130
Federalist, The, **4:**290, **4E:123;** **18:**1592, 1594
Federalists (Federalist Party), **3E:88;** **4:**290, 309,
        310, 313–14, **4E:**127, 143; **5:**370
    election of 1800 and, **4:**316
    election of 1804 and, **4:**338
    Jefferson and, **4:**316, 337, 338
    War of 1812 and, **4:**349
Federal Land Banks, **14:**1185
Federal Power Commission, **13:**1128
Federal Reserve System, **14:**1178, 1183
Federal Theater Project, **14:**1222
Felton, Rebecca L., **14E:489**

Fenno, John, **4E:123**
Ferdinand of Aragon, **1**:18–20, **1E:4**, **14**, *14*
Fermi, Enrico, **15E:**537
Fernandez de Enciso, Martin, **1E:4**
Ferraro, Geraldine, **18**:1569–70, *1570*, **18E:644–45**, *645*
Fessenden, William, **7**:610–11
Fetterman, Capt. William J., **9**:782, 792–93, **9E:310–11**
Feudal system, **1**:12
Field, Cyrus, **10**:*861,* 862, *863*; **11E:381–82**, *381*
Field, James G., **10**:856
Fifteenth Amendment, **8E:273–74**
"54 40' or fight," **6**:521–22
Fillmore, Millard, **7**:554, **7E:237–38**, *238*
Films, *see* Movies
Finney, Charles G., **6**:492, **6E:200**
Firearms, *see* Weapons
Firestone, Harvey, **13**:*1164*
First Continental Congress, **3**:185, 251–52, **3E:82**
    see also Continental Congress
First Neutrality Act (1935), **14**:1221
First Scottsboro Case (*Powell vs. Alabama*), **14**:1216
    see also Scottsboro Boys
Firtchie, Barbara, **8E:275**
Fish, Hamilton, **8E:274**; **9E:299**, 331
Fisk, James (Jubilee Jim), **10**:862, 865, **10E:338–39**, **349**; **11**:905, 906
Fiske, John, **11**:959–60, **11E:382**
Fitzgerald, F. Scott, **13**:1159–60, *1160*, **13E:457–58**
Fitzpatrick, Thomas (Tom), **6E:200–1**
Five Civilized Tribes, **5E:179**
Flagg, James Montgomery, **13E:458**
Flatboats, **5**:407, *408–13, 416*
Fletcher, Adm. Frank Jack, **15**:1294, **15E:530**
Florida, **1**:38, **1E:28**, 29; **5E:179**
    American acquisition of, **5**:366
    colonial, **2**:105–6, 125, 128, 154
    Indians, **1**:*42, 72*
Foch, Marshal Ferdinand, **13**:1097, 1100, **13E:471**
Fokker, Anthony, **13**:1105
Fonck, Rene, **13**:*1116*
Football, **13E:460**
Foote, Andrew Hull, **8E:274**
Forbes, Charles R., **13**:1123
Force Bill, **5E:163–64**
Ford, Edsel, **13E:458**
Ford, Gerald, **1**:7; **17**:1482; **17E:604–5**, *605*; **18**:*1534*, **1535–41**
Ford, Henry, **9**:808; **12**:1059; **13**:*1162*, **1163–68**, *1164, 1166*, **13E:458,**
Ford, Henry, II, **13E:458**
Ford Foundation, **13E:458**
Fordney-McCumber Tariff, **13**:1127
Foreign policy
    early 19th-century

Foreign Policy, early 19th-century (*cont.*)
    French Revolution and, **4**:309–10, 312, 314, *315,* 338
    Jackson and, **5**:402–4
    Monroe Doctrine, **5:368–70**
    Napoleonic Wars, **4**:338–39
    South America, **5**:392–93
    late 19th-century, **12**:995–97
    20th-century
        Carter, **18:1544–47**
        dollar diplomacy, **12:1033–35**, **12E:424**
        Eisenhower Doctrine, **16E:565**
        isolationism, **13:1133–34**, **13E:479**; **14**:1220–21
        Reagan administration, **18:1564–69**
        Franklin D. Roosevelt, **14**:1217, 1226
        Truman Doctrine, **15E:538**; **16**:1360, **16E:591**
        Woodrow Wilson, **12**:1035–36
    see also specific presidents, countries, wars, and other topics
Forrest, Edwin, **6E:201**, *201*
Forrest, Nathan Bedford, **8E:274–75**
Forrestal, James Vincent, **16E:567**
Forsyth, John, **5E:164**
Fortas, Abe, **17E:605–6**, *605*
Fort Christina, **1**:48, **1E:26**
Fort Dearborn, **4E:123**
Fort Duquesne, **2**:*110–13, 133,* 133–34, **2E:51**
Fort Laramie, Treaty of, **6E:219**
Fort Laramie, **6**:*525,* 525–27, *526*
Fort Louisbourg, **2**:*131,* 131–32
Fort Moultrie, **3**:210
Fort Orange, **1**:47, **1E:14–15**
Fort Sumter, **7**:618–19
Forty-niners (California Argonauts), **6**:524, **6E:196**; **9**:730, 759
Foster, Stephen Collins, **6E:201–2**
Founding Fathers, **4:275–77**
Four Hundred, the, **12:1050–52**
Fourteen Points, **13**:1099–100, 1102
Fourteenth Amendment, **8**:702–4, 706, **8E:275**; **10**:826–27; **11**:912–13; **14**:1216; **18**:1597
Fox, Charles James, **3E:86–87**, *87*
Fox Indians, **6E:193**
France, **1**:61; **13**:1134; **16**:1390
    American Revolution and, **3**:195–96, **220–22**, *222–23, 240–41,* 264, **3E:81**, 84, 94–95, **97**, 103–4
    England and, **2**:125–36
    Jackson and, **5**:404–5, *404*
    Native Americans and, **2**:128–30
    Treaty of Morfontaine and, **4**:316
    in Vietnam, **17**:1445
    in World War I, **13**:1085, 1094, 1102
    in World War II, **15**:1266, 1268, 1302
    XYZ affair, **4**:314, *315*
    see also French and Indian War; French colonies; French Revolution

Francis Ferdinand, Archduke, **13**:1085, *1086*

Franco, Francisco, **14**:1225; **15**:1266, **15E:530–31,** *530*

Franklin, Benjamin, **2**:*159, 163*; **3**:190, *200–1,* 220, 226, 246, 252–54, *255,* **3E:87–88,** *87*; **4**:275, 352; **10**:818

Franklin, John Hope, **10**:815

Franklin, State of, **4**:281

Frazier-Lemke Act, **14**:1254

Frederick II, King of Prussia, **2E:52**

Fredericksberg, Battle of, **8**:647–48, *648*

Freedom March on Washington (1963), **16**:1423, *1423,* **16E:562**

Freedom of the press, in colonial America, **2E:74**

Freedom rides, **16**:1421, **16E:562**

Free enterprise, *see* Capitalism

Free land legislation, **10**:845

Freeman, Mary Eleanor Wilkins, **11E:382**

Freeman, Thomas, **6**:512

Freeport Doctrine, **7**:560, **7E:238**

Free Soilers (Free Soil Party), **7**:550–51, 554, **7E:238**

Free-soil legislation, **9:773–75**

"Free Speech" movement, **17**:1449

Fremont, John C., **6**:513–14, 517, 523, **6E:202,** *202*; **7**:558

French, Daniel Chester, **11**:973, **11E:382–83,** *383,*

French and Indian War, **2:134–36,** 109, *109–22,* **2E:52**

French colonies, **1:43–47,** 64; **2**:99, 105, 125–36, **2E:49,** 55, 57–59, 63

French East India Company, **1E:9**

French Revolution, **3**:*252–53,* **3E:86,** 95, 97, 103; **4**:309–12, 314, *315,* 338, **4E:123–24,** *124*

Freneau, Philip Morin, **3E:88**; **4**:310

Frick, Henry Clay, **10**:816, 830, **10E:349–50,** *349*; **13**:1104

Friedan, Betty, **17E:622,** *623*

Frobisher, Sir Martin, **1E:15,** *15*

Frock, Henry, **10**:867

Frontenac, Count Louis de, **2**:126, **2E:52**

Frontier, **2**:124
  end of, **9**:776
  see also West, the

Frost, Robert Lee, **16E:568,** *568*

Fugitive Slave Law, **7E:238–39**

Fulbright, James William, **14E:489**; **17**:1449, **17E:606,** *606*

Fuller, Alvan Tufts, **13E:458–59**

Fuller, Margaret, **6E:202**

Fulton, Robert, **4**:353, **4E:124–25,** *124*; **5**:377, *382–83*; **10**:818

Fundamental Constitutions of Carolina, **2**:100–1

Fundamental Orders of Connecticut, **2**:97, **2E:55**

Furman v. *Georgia,* **17E:599**

Furniture and furnishings, Victorian, **11**:*947–53, 956–57*

Fur trade, **1**:43–44, *44–45*; **2**:95, 102, 125, 129–30

Fusang, **1E:15**

G

Gadsden, James, **7E:239**

Gadsden Purchase, **7E:239**

Gag, Anton, **9**:*778*

Gagarin, Yuri, **16**:1417; **17**:*1486, 1487*

Gage, Gen. Thomas, **3**:185–87, *186,* **3E:88**

Gag Rule, **5E:164**

Gaines, Edmund, **4E:125**; **7**:545–46

Gallatin, Albert, **4**:333, *335,* **4E:125,** *125*

Galleons, **1E:15**

Garbo, Greta, **13**:*1125,* **13E:459,** *459*

Garcia, Calixto, **12E:418**

Gardner, Isabella Stewart, **11:979–88,** *981, 982, 985, 986,* **11E:383**

Garfield, Harry A., **13**:1098, **13E:459**

Garfield, James A, **10**:875, 877, *877,* **10E:350**

Garland, Hamlin, **11E:383**

Garner, John Nance, **14**:1180, 1181

Garraty, John A., **10**:891–98

Garrison, William Lloyd, **6**:491–93, **6E:203,** *203*

Garros, Roland, **13**:1105

Garvey, Marcus Moziah, **13E:459–60,** *460*

Gaspee (schooner), **2**:*165, 166,* **2E:52**

Gast, John, **9**:*800–1*

Gates, Gen. Horatio, **3**:222, 264, 265, 267, **3E:88,** *88*

Gates, John Warren, **10E:350–51**

Gatling, Richard Jordan, **9E:311**

Gatty, Harold, **14**:1212, *1213*

Gaza Strip, **17**:1451

Gemini space program, **17**:*1492–93,* **17E:596–97**

General Motors, **14**:1224

Genet, Edmond Charles (Citizen Genet), **4**:*308,* 310–12, **4E:125–26**

Genetic engineering, **17:1512–13**

George, Henry, **10**:826, **10E:351**

George, Milton, **10**:854, **10E:359**

George, Walter F., **14**:1249, **14E:494–95**

George II, King of England, **2**:105, **2E:53,** *53*

George III, King of England, **2**:*150,* 159, 169, **2E:53**; **3**:185, 186, 190, *192,* 226, **3E:89,** *89*

Georgia, **3**:254
  colonial, **2**:105–6, *107*
  Indians in, **5**:397–98

German immigrants, **10**:887, 889

Germantown, battle of, **3**:220, *220–21*

Germany, **12**:1026
  Nazi, **14**:1218, 1226; **15**:1265
    Holocaust, **16E:570**
  in World War I, **13**:1085–90, 1092–94
    air war, **13**:*1105–17*
    Versailles Treaty (1919), **13**:1102–3, **13E:476**

Germany (*cont.*)
  in World War II, **15:**1268, 1270–73, 1291–92,
    1301–5, 1296–97, **15E:**532–33
Geronimo, **9:**788, *788,* 797, **9E:311,** *311*
Gerry, Elbridge, **4:***287,* **4E:126,** *126*
Gershwin, George, **14:**1223, **14E:495,** *495*
Gershwin, Ira, **14E:**495
Gettysburg, Battle of, **8:***649–53,* 654, 718
Gettysburg Address, **8:***661,* **8E:275–76**
Ghent, **1:**14
  Peace of, *see* Peace of Ghent
Ghost Dance cult, **9:**799, **9E:312**
Gibbons vs. Ogden, **5:**372–73, *372–73,* **5E:164**
Gibbs, Josiah Willard, **10:**818
G.I. Bill of Rights, **16E:568**
Gibson, Charles Dana, **12E:418–19**
Gilbert, Sir Humphrey, **1:**71, **1E:15**
Gilded Age, **11:915–18**
  ostentation during, **11:907–9**
  religion during, **11:914–18**
  wealth during, **11:905–18**
Gilmer, John, **7:**612
Ginsburg, Douglas H., **18:**1575
Glasnost, **18:**1571
Glass, Carter, **14:**1255, **14E:495**
Glenn, John H., Jr., **17:***1491*
Glidden, Joseph, **9:**770
Glover, John, **3E:89**
Glyn, Elinor Sutherland, **13:**1159, **13E:460**
Godfrey of Bouillon, **1:***16*
Goethals, George Washington, **12E:419**
Gold (gold mining), **9:**725–40, *733–36,* **9E:306–7;**
    11E:385
  Black Friday and, **10:**865, **10E:338–39**
  cost of, **9:732–34**
  discovery of, **9:**730
  "git and git out" in, **9:**740
  Indian troubles and, **9:**735, 738–39
  instant cities and, **9:736–38**
  mineral frontier doubles back in, **9:738–40**
  Panic of 1893 and, **10E:361–62**
  Pike's Peak Hoax and, **9E:323**
  prospectors, **9:***724, 730–32, 734*
  silver vs., **10:880–81, 884–86,** 893–94
  stampede to the fields and, **9:730–32**
Goldberg, Arthur Joseph, **17E:606–7,** *607*
Golden spike, driving of, **10:***834–35*
Goldman, Emma, **12:**1055, **12E:419,** *419*
Gold Rush, **6E:**194, 196, 209, **203–4,** *203;* **7:***551,* 551
  Indians and, **9:**796
Gold standard, **14:**1180
Goldwater, Barry M., **16:**1426–27; **17E:607,** *607*
Gompers, Samuel, **10:**829, **10E:351,** *351;* **12:**1052,
    1053, *1055*
Gone With the Wind, **14:**1223, *1224,* **14E:504–5**
Good-Neighbor Policy, **15E:553**
Goodyear, Charles, **5E:164,** *164*
Gorbachev, Mikhail, **18:**1571, *1573,* **18E:645**

Gorgas, Josiah, **5:**448
Gorges, Sir Ferdinando, **1:**76, **1E:15–16**
Gospel of wealth, **11:962–63**
Gould, Jay, **10:***861,* 862, *863, 864,* 865, 872, *872,*
    10E:351–52, 338–39; **11:**905, *907*
Government, *see* Federal government; State
    governments
Grain Futures Trading Act, **13:**1130
Gramm-Rudman-Hollings Act, **18:**1563
Grange, Harold Edward, **13E:460–61**
Granger laws, **10E:352**
Granges, **10:**853, 854, *854,* 893, **10E:352,** *352,* 356
Grant, Ulysses S., **9E:**302, 304, 308; **10:875–77,**
    881, **10E:357;** **11:**905
  Civil War and, **8:**637–38, *649,* 649–50, *657,*
    671–73, *674–75,* 676–77, *677,* 680–81, *688,*
    691, 706, *707,* 708, *708,* **8E:276–77,** *276*
Grant, Orvil, **9E:308**
Granville, Lord, **9E:331**
Grasshoppers, **9:**773
Grattan, Lt. J. L., **6:**526
Gray, Patrick, **17:**1481
Great American Desert, **9:**759, 766, 774; **10:**821
Great Awakening, **2E:50,** 53
Great Britain (England), **13:**1134; **14:**1180; **18E:665**
  Alabama claims and, **9E:299**
  Aroostook War, **6E:189**
  Civil War and, **8:**647
  Clayton-Bulwer Treaty with, **6E:197–98;** **12:**1025
  colonies in America, **1:**48, **63–81;** **2:95–108,**
    124–36
    first popular government, **1:77–80**
    Indians, **1:**72, 74, 79–80
    merchants, **1:**66
    private enterprise, **1:80–81**
    success of England in establishing colonies,
      1:63–64, 66
    trading companies, **1:66–67**
    why Englishmen left home, **1:67–70**
    women, **1:**64, 66
    see also American Revolution; War of 1812
      and specific colonies
  France and, **2:125–36**
  French and Indian War and, **2:**134–36
  impressment of American seamen by, **4:**312–13,
    339, 339–40
  Jackson and, **5:**402–4
  Jay's treaty with, **4:**312–14
  late 19th-century relations with, **12:**995–97
  Monroe Doctrine and, **5:**368–69
  Napoleonic Wars and, **4:**338–39
  Oregon and, **6:**517–18, 522
  Panama Canal and, **12:**1025–26
  religious persecution in (17th century), **1:**56–57
  Spain and, **2:**124–25, 127–28, 130–31
  trade with
    Embargo Act, **4:**340–41, *342–43,* **4E:122**
    Non-Importation Act, **4:**339, **4E:138**

Great Britain (England), trade with (*cont.*)
  Non-Intercourse Act, **4:**341, 344, **4E:138**
  post-revolutionary era, **4:**280–81
  Treaty of Washington and, **9E:**331
  Venezuela claims and, **12E:**430
  in World War I, **13:**1085–90, 1092–94, 1102
  in World War II, **15:**1266, 1268–72, 1301, 1302, 1304
  War of 1812 with, **4:317,** *318–31,* **344–49,** *345, 346, 349,* **4E:138; 5:**365
    Indians and, **4:**344–47
  see also individual kings and prime ministers
Great Compromise, **18:**1591
Great Depression
  Hoover and, **14:1176–81**
  legislation, **14:**1183, 1185–86
  Roosevelt's Hundred Days and, **14:**1181–82
  see also New Deal; Roosevelt, Franklin Delano
Great Diamond Fraud, **9E:**312
Great Medicine Road, **6:**524
  see also Oregon Trail
Great Northern Railroad, **9:**805, 807, *807,* 808; **10:**821, 872
Great Society, **16:**1426
Great White Fleet, **12E:419–20**
Greeley, Horace, **6:**527; **7E:239–40,** *240;* **8:**708; **9:**726; **10E:**357, 877; **11E:**392
Green, William, **13E:**461
Greenback Party (later Greenback Labor Party), **10:**884, 885, 893, **10E:**352
Greenbacks, **10:**881, 884, 893
Greene, Gen. Nathanael, **3:**261, *266,* 267–68, **3E:90**
Greene, Mrs. Nathanael, **5:**443, 444
Greenglass, David, **16E:**584–85
Greenland Colony, **1E:16,** 17
Green Mountain Boys, **3E:89**
Gregorian calendar, **1E:16**
Gregory, John H., **9:**732
Grenada, **18:**1568, **18E:645–46**
Grenville, George, **2:***158,* 159, **2E:53**
Grenville, Sir Richard, **1E:16**
Grierson, Col. Benjamin H., **8E:277; 9E:**302
Grimké sisters, **7E:240,** *240*
Grissom, Virgil I. ("Gus") **17:**1492, **17E:**597
Gropper, William, **14:**1227, *1237*
Grundy, Felix, **5E:165**
Guadalcanal, **15:**1295–96, *1296*
Guadalupe Hidalgo, Treaty of, **6:**524, 528; **7:**549, **7E:254**
Guadeloupe, **1E:28**
Guerriere, **4:***319–21*
Guerrilla warfare, in American Revolution, **3:**261–68
Guiteau, Charles J., **10:**875, *876,* **10E:352–53**
Gulf of Tonkin Resolution, **17:1446–47,** 1449, **17E:608**
Guston, Philip, **14:**1227, *1236*
Guynemer, Georges, **13:**1105
Gyroscope, **12E:**437

H

Hadley's quadrant, **1E:**3
Hague Tribunal, **12E:**420
Haig, Alexander M., Jr., **18E:646–48,** *647*
Haig, Field Marshal Douglas, **13:**1094
Haish, Jacob, **9:**770
Haiti, **14:**1216; **18E:**648
Haldeman, H. R. "Bob," **17:**1481, 1484, **17E:**628–29
Hale, John Parker, **7:**554, **7E:240–41**
Hale, Nathan, **3E:90,** *90*
Hale, Sarah, **6E:**204
Half Breed Republicans, **11:**912
Half-way Covenant, **2E:53–54**
  see also Congregationalism
Halleck, Henry, **8:**644, 646, **8E:**277
Halsey, Adm. William F. "Bull," **15:**1298, 1300, 1306–9, *1307,* **15E:531–32**
Hamburg, **1:**14, *15*
Hamilton, Alexander, **3:**195, **3E:88; 4:***274,* 282, 284, 288, 290, 310, 313, 316, **4E:126–27,** *126;* **10:**884; **18:**1594, 1597
  Burr and, **4:**316, 337–38
  Jefferson and, **4:**303, 304, 307–9, 316
  Report on Manufactures, **5:**370, 423, 426
  as Secretary of the Treasury, **4:**302–9, *305*
Hamlin, Hannibal, **8E:**277
Hammond, George, **4:**312
Hammond, James Henry, **7:**587, **7E:**241
Hampton, Wade, **8E:**277
Hampton Court Conference, **1E:**8
Hancock, John, **2:**162; **3:**185, **3E:90–91,** *91*
Hancock, Winfield Scott, **8E:277–78**
Handy, William Christopher, **12E:**420
Hanna, Marcus (Mark), **10:**896; **12E:420,** *421*
Hanseatic League, **1:***15*
Hardee, William Joseph, **8E:**278
Harding, Chester, **6E:**204
Harding, Warren G., **13:**1104, **1119–24,** *1120,* **13E:461–62**
Harlan, John Marshall, **9E:312–13**
Harney, Col. William S., **6:**527, **6E:**204
Harper, Robert Goodloe, **6E:**204
Harriman, Edward H., **9:**776, **805–8; 10:***872–73,* **10E:**353; **11:**906
Harrington, Michael, **16:***1436*
Harris, Joel Chandler, **11E:**384
Harris, Patricia, **18:**1547
Harrison, Benjamin, **10:**880, **10E:354,** *354*
Harrison, William Henry, **4:**340, *340, 341,* 344, 347, **4E:145; 5E:165**
Harte, Bret, **11:**970, **11E:384–85,** *384*
Hartford Convention, **4E:127**
Hartley, Marsden, **14:***1228*
Harvard, John, **2E:**54
Harvard College, **2E:**54

Hassam, Childe, **13E:462**
Hassman, Carl, **9:**788, *789*
Hatch, Col. Edward, **9E:**302
Hauptmann, Bruno Richard, **14E:**501
Hawaii, **12:**995, *1010–11*, **12E:425–26**
  annexation of, **12E:420–21**
Hawkins, Sir John, **1:***70*, 70, **1E:16**
Hawthorne, Nathaniel, **5E:165–66,** *166*
Hay, John, **12:**1010, 1026, 1032–33, **12E:421–22**
Hayes, Rutherford B., **8:**708–10, **8E:278–79,** *278*;
    10:828, 848, 877, 884, 885; **11:**946
Hay-Herran Treaty, **12:**1025–26, **12E:422**
Haymarket Square Riot, **10E:354**
Hayne, Robert Young, **5E:166**
Hay-Pauncefote Treaty, **6E:**198; **12:**1025, **12E:422**
Hays, Mary Ludwig, *see* Molly Pitcher
Hays, William Harrison, **13E:462**
Hays Code, **13E:**462
Haywood, William D. (Big Bill), **10E:344**
Hearst, George, **9E:**307; **11E:385**
Hearst, William Randolph, **12:***996,* 998–99,
    12E:422–23, *422*
Heart transplants, **17:1513–14**
Heilbroner, Robert L., **12:**1071–78
Helena, Montana, **9:**738, 740
Hellman, Lillian, **14:**1222
Helper, Hinton Rowan, **7E:241**
Hemingway, Ernest, **13:**1160–61, *1161,* **13E:462–63**
Hendriks, **10:***878*
Henry, Andrew, **6E:189**
Henry, Edward Lamson, **10:**843, **10E:354–55**
Henry, Patrick, **2:**157, 166, 169, **2E:54,** *54*; **3:**190,
    193, 194, 251, 254, **3E:93; 4:**290
Henry III, King of Castile, **1:**37
Henry IV, King of France, **1:**43, **1E:16–17,** *17*
Henry VIII, King of England, **1:***66,* 67, **1E:8,** 17
Henry Street Settlement, **12E:442**
Henry the Navigator, Prince, **1:**18, *18,* **1E:17**
Herbert, Victor, **12E:423**
Herjulfson, Bjarni, **1E:17**
Herkimer, Nicholas, **3E:91**
Hessians, **3:**212, 214, *240,* **3E:91,** *91*
Heyn, Allen, **15:***1340,* 1341–48
Hickock, James Butler ("Wild Bill"), **9:**739–40,
    9E:313, *313*
Hicks, John D., **10:**852
Higginson, Francis, **2:**172, **2E:54**
Highways, *see* Roads and highways
Hill, Ambrose Powell, **8:***651,* 654, **8E:279**
Hill, Daniel Harvey, **8E:279**
Hill, James J. (Jim), **9:**776, **9E:313–14; 10:**872, *873*
  legend of, **9:803–8,** *805, 806*
Hill, Louis, **9:***806*
Hindenburg (dirigible), **14:***1222,* 1225
Hindenburg, Paul von, **15:**1265
Hine, Lewis Wickers, **12E:423**
Hirohito, Emperor, **15:**1274
Hiroshima, **15:**1309, 1310, **15E:538**

Hispaniola, **1:**11, 20, 40, **1E:4,** **17–18**
Hiss, Alger, **16:**1390, **16E:568–69,** *569*
History of Plymouth Plantation (Bradford),
    2:173–74
Hitler, Adolf, **13:**1102; **14:**1218, 1226; **15:**1265–66,
    1267, 1297, **15E:532–33**
Hoar, George, **11E:385**
Ho Chi Minh, **16:**1390; **17:**1445
Hoffa, James, **17E:608–9,** *608*
Hoffman, Julius, **17E:600**
Holbrook, Stewart H., **9:**803–8; **10:**816
Holland (the Netherlands), **1:**61; **2:**127; **3:**221;
    15:1268
  colonies, **1:**47–48, 64; **2:**99, 100, 102
    New Amsterdam, **1:**47, **1E:25,** *25*
  Separatists in, **1:**58
Holliday, Cyrus, **9:**776
Hollywood, *see* Movies
Hollywood Ten, the, **16E:569–70,** *569*
Holmes, Oliver Wendell, **11E:385–86,** *385*
Holocaust, **16E:570**
Holy Roman Empire, **1E:8**
Homeless in America, **18E:648–49**
Home Owners Loan Corporation, **14:**1185
Homer, Winslow, **11:***971,* 973, **11E:386,** *386*
Homestead Act (1862), **5:**397; **6:**456; **9:**769, 773,
    774, **9E:314; 10:**845, 847
Homesteaders, **9:766–67,** *768, 769, 771–75*;
    10:845–50, *849, 850*
  free-soil legislation and, **9:773–75**
  immigrants as, **9:**775, 804
  Indians as, **9E:309**
  prairies and, **9:769–70**
  weather and grasshopper problems, **9:772–73,**
    773
Homestead strike, **10:**829, 867, **10E:355**
Honduras, **1E:9; 12:**1035; **18:**1569
Hone, Philip, **5E:166,** *166*
Hood, John Bell, **8:**680, 683, 684, **8E:279**
Hooker, Gen. Joseph, **8:**648, 654, **8E:279–80**
Hooker, Thomas, **2:**176–77, **2E:54–55**
Hoover, Herbert, **10:**821; **13:**1098, *1120,* 1121,
    1125–27, *1127,* **13E:463–64,** *463;* **14:***1181,*
    1208, 1213, 1215
  economic crisis and, **14:1176–81, 14E:485**
Hoover, John Edgar, **13E:**455; **16E:570–71,** *570*
Hoover Commission, **13E:464**
Hopewell mounds, **1E:24**
Hopkins, Esek, **3E:91–92,** *92*
Hopkins, Harry, **14:**1185, **14E:486; 15:**1271,
    15E:533, *533*
Hopper, Edward, **14:**1227, *1234,* **14E:495–96,** *496*
Horry, Maj. Peter, **3:**264, 265
Horses
  introduction of, **1E:18,** *18*
  Pony Express, **4:324–25**
  roundup of, **9:***744–45*
House, Col. Edward M., **13:**1087–88

House, Edward Mandell, **13E:464**
House Committee on Un-American Activities,
  16:1390, **16E:569**
House of Burgesses, **1E:20**; **2E:55,** *55*
House of Morgan, *see* Morgan, J. P.
House of Representatives, **18**:1591
  Missouri Compromise and, **5**:375–76
  see also Congress, U.S.
House of Trade (*Casa de Contratación*), **1**:40, 41
Housing, late 19th century, **11**:943
Houston, David, **10**:891
Houston, Sam, **6**:519, 520, *521*; **7**:*564–65,* 615,
  7E:241–42, *242*
Howe, Elias, **5**:447, **5E:166–67,** *167*
Howe, Julia Ward, **8E:280,** *280*
Howe, William, **3**:209–13, 217, 219, **3E:92**
Howells, William Dean, **11**:965, 967, 970,
  11E:386–87
Huascar, **1E:3**
Huayna Capac, **1E:18**
Hubbard, Elbert Green, **12E:423**
Hudson, Henry, **1**:*46,* 47, *47,* **1E:18**
Hudson's Bay Company, **2**:132, **2E:55**; **9**:803–4
Hudson River, **1**:*46* (map), 47, *47*
Hughes, Col. Charles Evans, **13**:1089, *1120,* 1121,
  1134, **13E:4664–65**; **14**:1253–58
Huguenots, **1**:64, **1E:31**
Huitzilopochtli, **1E:4**
Hull, Cordell, **15**:*1273,* 1274, **15E:533–34**
Hull, Isaac, **4**:*319,* 347, **4E:127**
Hull, William, **4**:345–46, **4E:127,** *127*
Hull House, **11**:946
Human rights, **18**:1544
Humphrey, Hubert H., **16**:*1427*; **17**:1454, 1458,
  17E:609
Humphrey, William E., **14**:1254
Hundred Associates, **1**:43–44, **1E:31**
Hungary, **16**:*1392,* 1393
Hunt, E. Howard, **17**:1480, **17E:628**
Hunt, Richard Morris, **11E:387**
Hunter, George, **6**:512
Hurons, **1E:5,** 7
Hutchinson, Anne, **2**:97, 98, **2E:55–56,** *55*
Hutchinson, Thomas, **2**:156, 163–64, 166, **2E:56**
Hwui Shan, **1E:15**

I

Iacocca, Lee Anthony, **18E:649**
IBM (International Business Machines),
  15E:552–53; **17:1505–7**
ICC (Interstate Commerce Commission), **10E:353,**
  355; **13**:1128
Ickes, Harold Le Claire, **14E:496**
Idaho, gold in, **9**:732–33
Iliff, John W., **9**:765

Illegal aliens, **18E:649–50**
Illinois Central railroad, **5**:440–41, *441*
Immigrants (immigration)
  early 19th century, **5E:167**
  late 19th century, **10**:*885,* **886–89**; **11**:943, 945
  early 20th century, **12**:1049–50
  in 1920s, **13**:1152, 1155
  in 1980s, **18E:649–50**
  Chinese, **10**:833, 834, 888, **10E:341**
  Cuban refugees, **18**:1546–47, *1547*
  Ellis Island, **10E:**348, 348–49
  Federal Immigration Act of 1891, **10E:349**
  German, **10**:887, 889
  as homesteaders, **9**:775–76, 804
  illegal aliens, **18E:649–50**
  industrialization and, **5**:426
  Irish, **10**:834
    Molly Maguires and, **9E:319**
  Italian, **10**:*888*
  New, **10E:360**
  Norwegian, Swedish, and Russian, **9**:775–76
  railroad building and, **10**:833, 834, 888
  Vietnamese refugees ("boat people"), **18**:1546
  in Westward movement, **9**:775–76; **10**:849–50,
    851
Impressment of American seamen by Great Brit-
    ain, **4**:312–13, *339,* 339–40
Incas, **1**:*21,* **1E:3,** **18–19,** 21, 27, 34
Indentured servants, **1E:19**; **4**:276
Independence Hall (Philadelphia), **18**:*1595*
Independent National Party, *see* Greenback Party
India, **1E:11**
Indians (Native Americans), **2E:63**; **4**:283; **6**:*505*;
    10:815–30
  American Revolution and, **3E:80,** 81, 105, **106**
  Battle of Tippecanoe and, **4**:344
  Bureau of Indian Affairs, **9E:303**
  cattle drives and, **9**:755
  Christianity and, **2E:50–51**
    missionaries, **2E:41**
  in colonial America, **2**:66, 67, 95, 97, 98, 102,
    104, 105, 125, 128–30, *146,* **2E:57–58,** 64
  Dawes Severalty Act and, **9E:309**
  first contacts with Europeans, **1:20–22**
  Five Civilized Tribes, **5E:179**
  French and Indian War and, **2**:109, *109–22,*
    134–36
  in French colonies, **1**:46; **2**:*112–13,* 125, 128–30
  frontier and, **2**:124
  Ghost Dance cult and, **9E:312**
  gold mining and, **9**:735, 738–39
  Great Britain and
    end of alliance, **4E:145**
    War of 1812, **4**:344–47
  Iroquois, **2**:126; **3E:80**
  Jackson and, **5**:366, **396,** 397–98, **5E:158**; **9E:314**
  messiah of, **9**:799
  Mound Builders, **1E:24**

Indians (Native Americans) (cont.)
  Northwest Territory and, **4E:**132, **145**
  Plains, **6:***497–509,* 525–27, **6E:212–13**
  railroads and, **9:**799–800; **10:***838*
  Removal Act of 1830, **6E:214**
  slavery and, **2E:**63
  Spain and, **1:**30, 39–40, **1E:**30
  Supreme Court and, **5:**397
  taming the West and, **9:791–99,** *790, 793–95*
  treaties with, **3E:**110; **4:***310, 311,* **4E:**132
  Van Buren and, **5E:158**
  War of 1812 and, **4:**346, 347
  wars with, **9:***777–89,* **791–99,** **9E:**301, 302, 304,
      306–11, 315–18, 325–30, 333, *333*
    Black Hawk War, **6E:193**
    northern plains, **9:**796
    Southwest, **9:**796–97
    westward expansion and, **5:**397–98; **6:**457–58,
        461, 466–67; **9:726–27,** *727, 729*
  see also specific tribes and chiefs
Industrialization, **5:423–41, 5E:155–56, 166–67,**
      170–71, 183
  age of steel, **10:821–25**
  agriculture and, **8:***700*
  child labor and, **5:**427–28
  Civil War and, **5:**443–48; **8:**698, **8E:271**
  factory system, **5:**425–28
  highways and, **5:**428–32, *430, 431*
  immigration and, **5:**426
  invention and, **10:818, 820–21**
  labor and, **10:827–30,** *827–29*
  modern America and, **10:**830
  monopoly and, **10:**822–23
  problems of, **10:**824–25
  railroads and, **5E:160;** **10:**821–22, 825, *827–29,*
      830, *831–43*
  robber barons and, **10:***861–73*
  specialization and, **10:**822
  steam engines and, **5E:163**
  Whitney and, **5:**443–48, **5E:185**
  women and, **5:**427–28, *429*
Industrial Revolution, **5:**377, *377–89,* **5E:167;**
      11:947, 949
Industrial Workers of the World (IWW), **10E:345**
Industry
  deregulation of, **18E:641**
  in postrevolutionary era, **4:**307–9
  regulation of, **10:**826–27
  trade and, **4:**279–80
  see also Industrialization; *and specific industries*
      (e.g., Iron industry*)*
Inflation, in 1970s, **17:**1476–77
Ingersoll, Robert Green, **11:**916–17,**11E:387–88,** *387*
Inoculation, in colonial Massachusetts, **2E:60**
Insull, Samuel, **13:**1128–29, **13E:465**
Integration
  busing for, **17E:599**
  see also Civil rights; Segregation

Intermediate Nuclear Forces (INF) Treaty,
      18:1571, 1573; **18E:650**
International Bank for Reconstruction and Devel-
      opment, *see* World Bank
International Court of Justice, **15:**1320
International Red Cross, **9E:300**
Interstate Commerce Act, **10E:355**
Interstate Commerce Commission (ICC), **10E:**355,
      353; **13:**1128
Inventions, *see* Science, technology, and
      inventions
Iran, **18:**1550–51
  hostage crisis, **18:**1551, **18E:653–54**
  war with Iraq, **18:**1566–67
Iran-Contra affair, **18:**1574–75, **18E:650–53**
Ireland, **13:**1102
Irish immigrants, **10:**834
  Molly Maguires and, **9E:319**
"Iron curtain," **16:**1356, **16E:526**
Iron industry, **5:**426–47, *428*
Iroquois Indians, **1E:**5, 7; **2:**125, 126, 128, **2E:***56;*
      3E:80
Iroquois League, **2E:**40–41, **56**
Irrigation, **9:**770, 774; **10:**845
Irving, Washington, **5E:167–68**
Isabella of Castile, Queen of Spain, **1:**18–20,
      1E:14, *14*
Isolationism, **13:**1133–34, **13E:479;** **14:**1220–21
Israel, **17:**1451, **17E:618;** **18:**1544–45
Italian immigrants, **10:***888*
Italy, **13:**1102, 1134
  Ethiopia invaded by, **15:**1265
  in World War II, **15:**1291, 1296–98, 1301
Iwo Jima, **15:***1308,* 1308
Izard, Ralph, **2:***139*
Izzie and Moe, **13E:465,** *465*

J

Jack, Capt., **9:**798, **9E:304**
Jackson, Andrew, **4E:128,** *128;* **5:***390,* 391–93,
      5E:168–69, *168;* **6:**519, 520; **10:**884
  Bank of the United States and, **5:**401–2
  England and, **5:**402–4
  foreign affairs and, **5:**402–4
  Indians and, **5:**366, *396,* 397–98, **5E:158**
  land policy of, **5:**397
  personal characteristics of, **5:**405–6
  as president, **5:**393–94, *393, 396,* 396–406,
      400–5
  the South and, **5:**398–400
  spoils system and, **5:**393
  War of 1812 and, **4:**348, 349
Jackson, Helen Hunt, **9E:314**
Jackson, Jesse, **18E:654–55,** *654*
Jackson, Robert Houghwout, **15E:534–35,** *535*

Jackson, Gen. Thomas (Stonewall), **8:**642–43, *644,*
    645, 651, 652, 654, **8E:280–81**
Jackson, William H., **9:***764–65*
Jackson State College, **17:**1475
Jacob, Henry, **2:**171
James, Frank, **10:***839*
James, Henry, **11:**965, **11E:388,** *388*
James, Jesse Woodson **10:**839, **10E:355–56,** *355*
James, Maj. John, **3:**264
James, William, **11E:388–89,** *389*
James I, King of England, **1:**49, *60,* 61, 69, 70, 73,
    1E:19, *19*
James II (Duke of York), King of England, **2:**102,
    2E:56–57
Jamestown, **1:**70, 74, 75, **1E:20,** 33
Janin, Henry, **9E:**312
Japan, **6E:**211–12; **12:**1029; **13:**1134 **14:**1213, 1216,
    1221, 1226; **15:**1265
    Panay incident, **14E:506–7,** *506*
    war with Russia, **12:**1032–33
    in World War II, **15:**1274, **1291–96, 1298–1301,**
    1298, 1299, **1305–10,** 1333, **15E:**537–38
    after World War II, **16:**1362, 1364
Jaworski, Leon, **17:**1483, **17E:**628–29
Jay, John, **4:***274,* 290, 302, 304, *312,* 312–13,
    4E:128–29, *128*
Jay's Treaty, **4E:129**
Jeannette Disaster, **9E:**314
Jefferson, Thomas, **2:**166; **3:**190–94, **197–208,**
    200–1, 247, 250, **3E:92–93,** *92;* **4:**282–83,
    291–99, **4E:129–30,** *130;* **18:**1589
    federal government role and, **4:**302–3, 307, 309
    French Revolution and, **4:**310–12
    Hamilton and, **4:**303, 304, 307–9, 316
    Monroe Doctrine and, **5:**369
    Peale and, **4:**352
    as president, **4:**316, 333–41
        Embargo Act, **4:**340–41, *342–43*
        Louisiana Purchase, **4:**335–36
        Tripolitan War, **4:**332, **4E:***116* (map)
        the West and, **4:**336–37
    Eli Whitney and, **5:**447
Jehovah's Witnesses, **9E:**327
Jenkins, Capt. Robert, **2:**130
Jenkins' Ear, War of, **2E:57**
Jenney, William, **11E:389**
Jenson, Oliver, **4:**351–58
Jesuits, **1E:**5
Jewett, Sarah Orner, **11E:389–90**
Jews
    in colonial America, **2E:**73
    Holocaust, **16E:**570
    in Supreme Court, **14E:**487, 489–90; **17E:**605–6
Jobs, Steven, **17:***1507,* 1507
Jodl, Gen. Adm., **15:**1305
Johnny Appleseed, *see* Chapman, John
John Paul II, Pope, **18E:655–56**
Johns, Jasper, **16:***1377*

Johnson, Andrew, **7:***614, 615;* **8:**697, 701,
    702–5, **8E:281–82,** *281;* **10:**875
    impeachment proceedings against, **8:***704–5,*
    705–6
Johnson, Eastman, **12E:423–24**
Johnson, Gerald W., **7:**621–28
Johnson, Herschel V., **7:**609
Johnson, Hugh Samuel, **14:**1186, 1241, **14E:496–97**
Johnson, Sir John, **3E:93**
Johnson, John A. ("Jack"), **12E:424**
Johnson, Lyndon Baines, **1:**6; **16:**1424, 1426, 1427,
    1427, **16E:**571; **17:***1450,* **17E:610–11,** *611*
    Vietnam War and, **17:**1446, 1447, 1449, 1452–53
Johnson, Richard M., **5E:169**
Johnston, Gen. Albert Sidney, **6:**527, 528,
    6E:194–95; **8:**638, 676, 678, 680, **8E:282**
Johnston, Joseph Eggleston, **8E:282**
Johnstown Flood, **9E:**315
Jolson, Al, **13:**1158, *1159,* **13E:465–66;** **14:**1209
Jones, John Paul, **3:**224, *224,* **3E:93–94,** *93*
Jones, Robert Tyre (Bobby), Jr., **14:**1211, *1212,*
    14E:497
Jones, Commodore Thomas ap Catesby, **7:**546,
    7E:242
Jones, William R., **12E:424**
Jordan, **17:**1451
Jordan, Vernon, Jr., **18:**1552
Joseph, Chief, **9:**798–99, *798,* **9E:315,** *315*
Josephson, Matthew, **10:**861, 881
Juan Carlos, King of Spain, **15E:**531
Judicial branch, **4:**288, 304; **18:**1597–98
Judson, Edward Z. C., *see* Buntline, Ned

K

Kalakaua, King of Hawaii, **12E:425–26**
Kalb, Johann, **3E:94**
Kane, John, **10:***820,* **10E:356**
Kansas, **7:**555–57
Kansas-Nebraska Act, **7:**556, 557, **7E:242,** *243*
Kansas Pacific Railroad, **10:**821
Karlsefni, Thorfinn, **1E:20**
Karp, Walter, **17:**1519–28
Kearny, Gen. Stephen W., **6:**523; **7:**549, *568,*
    7E:243
Keats, John, **1E:**11
Keelboats, **5:**407, *408–13*
Kefauver, Carey Estes, **16E:571–72,** *571*
Kehoe, Jack, **9E:**319
Kelley, Oliver H., **10:**853, **10E:356**
Kelley-Bessemer process, **10:**816
Kellogg, Frank Billings, **13E:466;** **14:**1211, **14E:497**
Kellogg-Briand Pact (1928), **13:**1134, **13E:466**
Kelly, Ellsworth, **16:***1376*
Kendall, Amos, **5E:169,** *169*
Kennedy, Edward Moore (Ted), **17E:612**

Kennedy, John Fitzgerald, **1:**6; **16:***1414,* 1415–18, 1422–24, *1428,* **1429–38,** *1431, 1432, 1435, 1436,* **16E:572–74,** *572;* **17:**1446
  assassination of, **16:**1424; **17E:627–28**
Kennedy, Joseph Patrick, **14E:497–97**
Kennedy, Robert Francis, **16:***1428;* **17:**1449, 1454, 1456, **17E:612–13,** *613*
Kensington Stone, **1E:20–21,** *20*
Kent State University, **17:1475–76,** *1476,* **17E:613**
Kentucky and Virginia Resolutions, **18:**1589–90
Kerrigan, Jimmy, **9E:319**
Kesselring, Field Marshal Albert, **15:**1297, 1298, 1301
Key, Francis Scott, **4:***330,* 348, **4E:130**
Khomeini, Ayatollah Ruhollah, **18:**1551
Khrushchev, Nikita S., **16:**1392, 1417, *1435*
King, Clarence, **9E:312**
King, Martin Luther, Jr., **16:**1422–24, *1422, 1423,* **16E:***574,* 562; **17:**1454, 1456, *1456, 1457,* **17E:613–14**
King, Richard, **9E:316**
King, Rufus, **4E:130,** *130*
King George's War (War of the Austrian Succession), **2:**109, 131–32, **2E:57**
King Philip's War, **2E:57–58,** *58*
King William's War, **2:**109, 126–17, **2E:58**
Kinkaid, Adm. Thomas Cassin, **15:**1306, 1307, **15E:535**
Kintpuash, *see* Jack, Capt.
Kiowas, **9:**796–97, **9E:327–28**
Kirkland, Lane, **16E:558**
Kissinger, Henry Alfred, **17:**1474, 1482, 1483, **17E:614–15**
Kittson, Norman Wolfred, **9:**803–4, **9E:316**
Kleindienst, Richard G., **17:**1481
Kline, Franz, **16:***1374–75*
Knights of Labor, **10:**828–29, **10E:356,** 368
Know-Nothing Party, **7E:243;** **10:**887
Knox, Henry, **3E:94,** *94*
Knox, Philander Chase, **12:**1034–35, **12E:424,** *424*
Knox, Wilson Franklin (Frank), **14E:498–99,** *498;* **15:**1274
Korea, **12:**1033; **15E:523**
Korean War, **15E:537;** **16:1386–90,** *1388, 1389,* **16E:574–75**
Kosciusko, Thaddeus, **3E:94,** *94*
Kosygin, Aleksei, **17:**1450, *1450,* **17E:597**
Krimmel, John Lewis, **5E:169**
Kublai Khan, **1E:28**
Kuhn, Loeb & Company, **9:**806
Ku Klux Klan, **8:707, 8E:282–83;** **10:**887, 898; **13:**1156, *1157*
Kunstler, William, **17E:600**
Kurile Islands, **15:**1333
Kurita, Adm. Takeo, **15:**1307–9
Kurusu, Saburo, **15:***1273,* 1274

Labor, **10:827–30,** *827–29*
see also Workers
Labor unions (organized labor), **5:**428
  in late 19th-early 20th century, **10:***824,* **827–30,** *827–29;* **12:**1052–53
  in 1920s, **13:1131–33**
  in 1930s, **14:1223–25,** 1247
  AFL-CIO (American Federation of Labor-Congress of Industrial Organizations), **16E:558,** 577, 578, 583
  American Federation of Labor (AFL), **10:**829, **10E:337,** 351; **12:**1053; **13:**1131–32, **13E:461;** **14:**1223–24, **14E:500**
  Committee for Industrial Organization (later the Congress of Industrial Organizations; C.I.O.), **13E:461;** **14:**1223–24, **14E:500**
  Taft-Hartly Act and, **16E:589–90**
  after World War II, **16:**1358, 1359
  see also specific labor unions and labor leaders
Ladd, William, **6E:204–5,** *205*
Lafayette, Marquis de, **3E:94–95,** *95;* **4:***278–79*
Lafayette Escadrille, **13:***1108–9*
Laffite, Jean, **4E:130–31**
Lafollette, Robert Marion, **12E:424–25,** *425;* **13:**1124, **13E:479**
La Guardia, Fiorello H., **14:**1218–19, *1246,* **14E:499**
laissez faire, **10:**824
Lake Champlain, **2:***116*
Lake George, Battle at, **2:***114–15*
Lancaster Turnpike, **5:**430–31, **5E:169–70**
Land Act of 1820, **6E:204–5,** *205*
Landon, Alfred M., **14:**1244–45, **14E:499,** *499*
Land policy, **4:**285
  American Revolution and, **3:**247–50
  grants to railroads, **10:**852, *853* (map)
  Homestead Act of 1862, **5:**397
  Jackson's, **5:**397
Landsdale, Nelson, **11:**979–88
Lane, Joseph, **7:**609, **7E:243–44**
Lane, Sir Ralph, **1:**72, **1E:21**
Langley, Samuel Pierpont, **12E:425**
Laos, **17E:610**
Lardner, Ring, **16E:569**
Larkin, Thomas, **6:**522, **6E:205**
La Salle, Robert Cavelier de, **2:**105, 125, **2E:58–59,** *58*
Lasers, **17:**1511
Las Salinas, Battle of, **1E:3**
Latin America
  colonial, **2:**130
  dollar diplomacy and, **12:1033–35,** **12E:**424
  Good Neighbor policy toward, **15E:553**
  late 19th-century policy toward, **12:**996–97
  Monroe Doctrine and, **5:**368–70
  Pan-American Union, **12E:430–31**

L

Latin America (*cont.*)
    Spanish colonies in, **1:40–43,** 48, 64, 70; **2:**130
        Indians, **1:**40, **1E:**30
        Line of Demarcation, **1E:**21, *21* (map)
        see also specific colonies
    trade with, **5:**392–93
    see also Central America; *specific countries*
Latrobe, Benjamin, **5E:170**
Laughs Kills Lonesome (Russell), **9:***746–47*
Laurens, Henry, **3E:95; 4E:131**
Lawrence, Ernest O., **14:**1215, **14E:499–500,** *500*
Lawrence, Capt. James, **4:***326–29, 332*
Lazarus, Emma, **10:**887, **10E:356–57**
League of Nations, **13:**1099–104, 1120, 1133,
       13E:467, 476; **14:**1211, 1213, 1218; **15:**1265
Leahy, William Daniel, **15E:535–36,** *536*
Lease, Mary Elizabeth, **10:**856, **10E:357**
Lebanon, **16:**1394; **18:**1539, 1544, 1564–65
Ledyard, John, **4E:131,** *131*
Ledyard, William, **3E:95**
Lee, Gen. Charles, **3:**210, **3E:95**
Lee, Col. Henry, **3:***266,* **3E:96**
Lee, Richard Henry, **3:**190, **3E:96,** *96;* **4:**278, 290
Lee, Robert E., **7:***573;* **8:**642–48, 651–52, 654, *666,*
       671–73, 676–78, 680, 681, *682, 683,* 684, *680,*
       681, 716, **8E:283–84**
Leigh, W. R., **9:***786–87*
LeMay, Gen. Curtis, **16E:**559; **17:**1454
Lendlease program, **15:**1269–70
L'Enfant, Pierre Charles, **4E:131–32**
Leonov, Aleksei A., **17:**1493
Leopold I, **2:**127
Lesueur, Charles, **6E:205**
Leuchtenburg, William E., **16E:**1429–38
Levant Company, **1:**66–67
Lewis, John L., **13E:**461; **14:***1223,* 1225, **14E:500;**
       16E:575–76, *576*
Lewis, Capt. Meriwether, **4:**291, 336; **6:**511–12,
       512–13, **6E:205–6,** 206
Lewis, Sinclair, **13:**1159, *1160,* **13E:466,**
Lewis, William B., **5E:170**
Lewis and Clark expedition, **4:**291; **6E:205–6,** *206*
Lexington, Battle of, **3:**185–86, 189, **3E:**84, 88, 91,
       98
Liberal Republican Party, **10:**877, **10E:357**
Liberia, **6E:**188–89
Liberty League, **14:***1243,* 1244–45, **14E:500–1**
Liberty Party, **6:**493, **6E:206–7**
Libya, **18:**1566, **18E:656–57,** *656*
Lichtenstein, **16:***1380–81*
Liddy, G. Gordon, **17:**1480, **17E:628**
Lie, Jonas, **13E:466–67**
Liliuokalani, **12E:425–26**
Lily, The, **6E:193**
Lincoln, Abraham, **1:**8; **6:**491; **7:***608, 613,* **7E:244;**
       8E:284–85, *284,* **9:**779, **9E:**300, 323; **10:**833;
       11:973, **11E:382–83**
    assassination of, **8:***662–65,* 684, **8E:264**

Lincoln, Abraham (*cont.*)
    Civil War and, **8:**635, 642, 645, 647, 648, 654,
       655, *655–62,* 679–80
    debates with Douglas, **7:**560, **7E:244–45**
    election of 1860, **7:**609–11
    Emancipation Proclamation, **8:***660,* **8E:271–72**
    Gettysburg Address, **8:**661, **8E:271–72**
    reconstruction and, **8:**698–700
Lincoln, Gen. Benjamin, **3:**263, 264, **3E:96,** *96*
Lincoln Plan (One-Tenth Plan), **8:**700
Lind, Jenny, **6:***488–89,* **6E:207,** *207*
Lindbergh, Charles A., **14:**1209, 1213–15,
       14E:501–2, *501*
Line of demarcation, **1E:21,** *21* (map)
Linotype, **10E:358**
Literature
    19th century, **5E:161–62,** 165–68; **6:**495, **6E:198**
    1880s-1890s, **11:964–67,** 970–72
    1920s, **13:**1159–61
    1930s, **14:**1222
    dime novels, **9E:**302–3
    women and, **5E:172–73**
    see also individual authors
Little Big Horn River, Battle of (Custer's Last
       Stand) **9:**785, *786–87,* 796, **9E:308–9,** *308*
Little Crow, **9:***778,* 779, **9E:316**
Little Rock (Arkansas), **16:**1420
Little Turtle, **4E:132,** *132*
Little Wolf, **9E:316–17,** *316*
Litvinov, Maxim, **14:**1216, 1217; **15:**1266
Livingston, Robert, **3:**190, *200–1,* **3E:97;** **4:**335,
       336, *336;* **5:**366
Livingstone, David, **11E:398–99**
Lloyd, Henry D., **10:**826, **10E:357–58**
Lloyd George, David, **13:**1093, 1100, 1101, *1103,*
       13E:467
Locke, John, **2:**100, **2E:59,** *59;* **3:**191, 246
Lodge, Henry Cabot, **12:**995, 1005; **13:**1104,
       13E:467–68, *467*
London, **1:**14
    Elizabethan, **1:50–53**
London, Jack, **12E:426,** *426*
London Company, **1:**67, 73–77
Long, Huey, **14:***1217,* 1220, **14E:502**
Long, John D., **12:**1006
Long, Maj. Stephen H., **6:**512, 513, **6E:207**
Longfellow, Henry Wadsworth, **2E:**40, 41, 68;
       11E:390
Longstreet, James, **8:**654, **8E:285**
Louis, Morris, **16:***1373*
Louisiana, **2:**105, *125*
Louisiana Purchase, **4:**291, 292, *293,* 335–36, *337*
       (map), **4E:132; 5:**366–67; **6:**468
Louis XIV, King of France, **1:**44; **2:**127, **2E:59**
Louis XVI, King of France, **3E:97,** *97*
Louis Philippe, King of France, **4E:132–33,** *133;*
       5:404
Love Canal, **17:**1515; **18:**1549

Lovell, James A., **17E:**597
Lowell, Abbott Lawrence, **13E:468**
Lowell, James Russell, **11E:390–91**, *390*
Loyalists, American Revolution and, **3:**189, 193–94, 210, 248–49, **3E:**93, **97–98**; **4:**281
Ludendorff, Erich von, **13:**1094
Luke, Frank, **13:***1117*
Lumbermen, **10:**846, *847*
Lundy, Benjamin, **6E:207**
Lusitania, **13:***1087,* 1088, **13E:468**
Luther, Martin, **1E:**8

M

McAdoo, William Gibbs, **13E:468–69**, *469*
MacArthur, Gen. Douglas, **14E:**486; **15:**1292, 1298, 1300, 1306, 1307, *1307*, **15E:536–37**; **16:**1362
  Korean War and, **16:**1387–88, **16E:590–91**
McAuliffe, Christa, **18:**1573
McCarthy, Eugene J., **17:**1454, **17E:616–17**, *617*
McCarthy, Joseph R., **13E:**453; **16:**1390–92, *1391*, **16E:576–77**, *576*
McClellan, Maj. Gen. George B., **8:**636–67, 639, *639,* 642–44, *643,* 683, 718, **8E:285**
McClure, Samuel Sidney, **12E:427**
McCord, James, **17:**1480, **17E:**628
McCormick, Cyrus, **5:**384–85, 447, **5E:170–71**, *170*; **10:**848
McCormick Harvesting Machine Company, **10:**828
McCoy, Joseph G., **9:**761, **9E:317**
McCrady, John, **14:***1232*
McCulloch vs. Maryland, **5:**371–72, **5E:171**; **7:**624–25
McDivittt, James A., **17:***1493*
McDowell, Brig. Gen. Irvin, **8:**636
Macedonian, **4:***322–23*
McGann, Thomas F., **1:**83–88
McGovern, George S., **17:**1479–80, **17E:617**, *617*
McGuffey, William Holmes, **6E:207–8**
Machine-age culture, **11:959–77**
Machu Picchu, **1E:**21
Mackay, John W., **9E:**307
Mackenzie, Ranald Slidell, **9E:317**
McKinley, William, **10:***858–59,* 859, 860, 896; **12:**997, 998, 1003, 1006, 1007, 1010–12, 1025, **12E:427–28**, *427*
McKinley Tariff (1890), **10:**880, 885, **10E:358**
McLane, Louis, **5E:171**
Maclay, William, **4E:133**
McNamara, James B. and John J., **10E:**344
McNamara, Robert S., **16:***1432,* **16E:577**, *577*
McNary-Haugen Farm Relief Bill, **13:**1130
Macon, Nathaniel, **4E:133**
Macon's Bill No. 2, **4:**344, **4E:133**
McParlan, James, **9E:**319, 323
McPherson, Aimee Semple, **14E:502–3**, *502*

Macready, William Charles, **6E:**199
McReynolds, James C., **14:**1254, **14E:503**
Madison, Dolley, **4E:133–34**, *134*
Madison, James, **3:**256; **4:***274,* 284–87, 290, 302, 304, 311, **4E:134–35**, *134*; **5:**365, 366; **18:**1589, 1592–94, 1597
  Monroe Doctrine and, **5:**369
  as president, **4:**338, **341–9**
    War of 1812, **4:344–49**
Magazines, **13:**1159
Magellan, Ferdinand, **1:**37–38, **1E:21–22**
Mahan, Alfred Thayer, **12E:428**
Mahone, William, **8:***676*
Mail service, Pony Express, **9E:**324–25
Mailer, Norman, **16:**1429–30
Maiman, Theodore Harold, **17:**1512
Maine, **1:**72; **6E:**189
  colonial, **2:**97
Maine, U.S.S., **12:***1000–1,* 1004–5, **12E:428**
Malcolm X, **16E:**562; **17E:615–16**, *615*
Manchuria, **12:**1035; **15:**1265
Mandan Indians, **6:***502, 506,* 506, *508–9*
Mandela, Nelson, **18E:**664
Mangas Coloradas, **9:**797, **9E:317–18**
Manhattan, **4:**336
  purchase of, **1E:**22
Manhattan Project, **14E:**500; **15E:537–38**, *537*; **16E:**580
Manifest Destiny, **6:**515, **6E:208**, 211
Mann, Horace, **5E:171–72**, *171*; **6:**494
Mann Act, **12:**1055–56, **12E:428–29**
Mannock, Edward "Mick," **13:***1116*
Manufacturing, *see* Industry
Mao Tse-tung, **15E:**525; **16:**1385; **17:**1478; **18:**1
Marbury vs. Madison, **5:**370, **5E:172,**
March on Washington (1963), **16:**1423, *1423,* **16E:**562
Marconi, Guglielmo, **12:**1062
Marcos de Niza, *see* Niza, Marcos de
Marcy, William L., **7E:245**
Maria Theresa, Queen of Austria, **2:**131
Marin, John, **14:***1235*
Marion, Francis (Swamp Fox), **3:**196, *260,* **261–68**, *263, 265,* **3E:**97
Marne, Battle of the (1918), **13:**1094
Marquette, Jacques, **2E:**59
Marquette, John, **2E:**57
Mars, **17:***1501*
Marsh, Reginald, **14:**1227, *1233,* **14E:503**
Marshall, Gen. George C., **15E:538–39**; **16:**1360, 1391
Marshall, James, **6:**469, *471,* 524
Marshall, John, **5:**370–74, *371–73, 375,* 397, **5E:172,** *172*; **18:**1598
Marshall, Thurgood, **17E:616,** *616*
Marshall Plan, **15E:538–39**; **16:***1359,* 1360
Martin, Fletcher, **14:***1237*

Martin, Josiah, **3E:97–98**
Martin, Thomas S., **14E:**495
Martineau, Harriet, **5E:172–73,** *173*
Maryland, **3:**248
  colonial, **2:**99–100, *101,* **2E:**46
Mason, George, **3E:98; 4:***287*
Mason, James Murray, **7E:245–46,** *246*
Mason, John Y., **7E:246**
Mason and Dixon Line, **7E:246**
Massachusetts
  American Revolution and, **3:**185–87, *188–89,*
    189, **3E:**82
  colonial, **1:**77; **2:**95–96
  constitution of, **3:**247
Massachusetts Bay Company, **2:96–99,** 171, 173,
  2E:59–60
Massasoit, Chief, **1:**80, **1E:22; 2E:**73
Masters, Edgar Lee, **12E:429**
Mather, Cotton, **2E:60,** *60*
Mather, Increase, **2E:60–61**
Mather, Richard, **2E:61,** *61*
Mauchly, John, **17:**1505
Maverick, Samuel, **9:**760
Mavericks, **9:**760
Mayflower, **1:***61,* 77, **1E:22–23,** *22;* **2:**173, 174
Mayflower Compact, **1:***78,* 79, **1E:23; 2:**96
Mayo, William, **9E:**309
Meade, George Gordon, **8:***652–53,* 654, 671, 697,
  8E:285–86
Meany, (William) George, **16E:577–78,** *578*
Meat-packing industry, **10:**817, *819*
Media, *see* Magazines; Newspapers; Radio;
  Television
Medicare and Medicaid, **17E:617–18**
Meir, Golda, **17E:618**
Mellon, Andrew William, **13:**1104, 1121; **14:**1177,
  14E:503–4, *503*
Melville, George Wallace, **9E:**314
Melville, Herman, **2E:**64; **7E:246–47,** *246*
Mencken, H. L., **10:**891
Mendoza, Antonio de, **1:**42, **1E:23,** *23*
Menendez de Aviles, Pedro, **1E:**31
Mennonites, **9E:318,** *318*
Mentally ill, the, **6E:**199
Mercantilism, **1E:23**
Mercer, Hugh, **3E:98**
Merchant Marine Act of 1920, **13:**1127–28
Merchants, 15th-16th century, **1:**12, 17
Mergenthaler, Ottmar, **10E:358**
Merrimack, see *Monitor* and *Merrimack,* Battle of
  the
Merry Mount, Ma., **2:**95, 96
"Message to Garcia, A," **12E:429**
Mexican War, **6:**523–24, 528; **7:545–50,** *561–79*
  Treaty of Guadalupe Hidalgo, **6:**524, 528; **7:**549,
  7E:254
Mexico, **5E:152; 7:**550; **13:**1090, **13E:**471
  California and, **6:**522, 523

Mexico (*cont.*)
  colonial, **1:**42–43, **1E:**10–11
  Texas and, **6:**519–20
  see also Aztecs
Miami Indians, **4E:**132
Middle East, **16:**1393–94; **17:**1451
  energy crisis of 1970s, **18:**1542
  "shuttle diplomacy," **18:**1539
Midway Island, Battle of, **15:**1294–95, *1294*
Midwest, the, **6:**468
  see also West, the
Migrant laborers, **16:**1416, 1426; **17E:**599; **18E:**650
Miles, Col. Nelson A., **9:***785,* 796, **9E:318–19**
Miller, Alfred Jacob, **6E:**208
Milling methods, **10:**848–49
Millis, Walter, **14:**1221, **4E:504,**
Mining
  gold, *see* Gold
  Molly Maguires and, **9E:**319
  placer, **9E:**324
  of silver, **9:**731, 740
Minnesota massacre, **9:***778–79*
Minnesota Rate Case, **10:**827
Minuit, Peter, **1E:23–24**
Minutemen, **3E:98,** *98*
Miranda ruling, **16E:**592; **17E:618–19**
Missionaries, Native Americans and, **2E:**41
Missionary Ridge, Battle of, **8:**673, *674–75*
Mississippi River, **1:**84; **2:***125*
Mississippi Valley, **2:**105
Missouri Compromise, **5:**375–76, 391–92, **5E:173,**
  173; **7:**552, 555, 558–60, **7E:**237
Mitchell, John, **17:**1480
Mitchell, Margaret, **14:**1223, **14E:504–5,** *504*
Mitchell, William Lendrum (Billy), **14E:505,** *505*
Model Cities program, **16:**1426
Modocs, **9:**797–98, *797,* **9E:**304
Mohawk Indians, **2E:**64; **3E:**80
Molasses Act (1733), **2:**153, 155
Moley, Raymond, **14:**1239, **14E:**486
Molly Maguires, **9E:319**
Molly Pitcher, **3E:98–99,** *99*
Mondale, Walter F., **18:**1540, 1569–70, *1570,*
  18E:657
Mongolian People's Republic, **15:**1333
Monitor and *Merrimack,* Battle of the, **8E:286,** *286*
Monopolies, **10:**822–23
  Clayton Antitrust Act and, **12:**1053, **12E:414**
  Sherman Antitrust Act and, **10:**826, **10E:366–67;**
  12E:414
  see also Trusts
Monroe, James, **4E:135,** *135*
Monroe, Marilyn, **16:***1408*
Monroe Doctrine, **5:**368–70, **5E:173–74**
  Lodge Corollary to, **13E:**467
  Roosevelt Corollary to, **12:**1028, **12E:433–34**
Montana, gold in, **9:**733–40
Montcalm, Marquis Louis Joseph de, **2:***119,* **2E:61**

Monterde, Gen. Jose Mariano, 7:*576*

Montevideo Conference (1933), **14**:1217

Montezuma, **1**:*30,* 34, **1E**:4, **24,** *24*

Montgomery (Alabama) bus boycott, **16E**:562

Montgomery, Gen. Bernard L., **15**:1296, 1304, 1305, **15E:539,** *539*

Montgomery, Richard, **3E:99**

Montgomery, Lt. Zebulon, **6**:512–13

Monticello, **4E:135–36,** *135*

Moody, Dwight Lyman, **11**:917–18, **11E:391,** *391*

Moon exploration, **17**:*1492–1500*

Mooney, Thomas, **13E**:478

Moore, James, **3E:99**

Morfontaine, Treaty of (Convention of 1800), **4**:316, **4E**:120

Morgan, J. P., **9**:776, 805, 806; **10**:818, *868–69,* 872, **10E:358–59,** *358*

Morgan, J.P., Company (House of Morgan), **10E**:359, 858

Morgan, John Hunt, **8E:286–87**

Morgenthau, Henry, Jr., **15E:539–40**

Morison, Samuel Eliot, **2**:178

Mormons, **6**:524, 527–29, *528–29,* **6E**:194, **208–9,** *208,* **215–16, 222; 9**:725, 730

Morrill Tariff of 1861, **10**:879, **10E:359**

Morris, Gouverneur, **4E:136**

Morris, Richard B., **18**:1589–98

Morris, Robert, **3E:99–100,** *100*

Morse, Samuel F. B., **5E:174,** *174*

Morton, Thomas, **2**:95, 96, **2E:61**

Mosby, John Singleton, **8E:287**

Mott, Lucretia, **6E:209**

Moultrie, Col. William, **3**:210, *212,* **3E:100**

Mound builders, **1E:24,** *24*

Mt. St. Helens volcano, **18**:1550

Mount Vernon, **4E:136**

Movies

  in 1920s, **13**:1148–49, 1158

  in 1930s, **14**:1221

  in 1950s, **16**:1395, *1400–9*

  animated cartoons, **14**:1209, *1211,* **14E:491–92**

  Hays Code, **13E**:462

  Hollywood Ten, **16E:569–70**

Muckrakers, **12**:1053, 1055

  see also Baker, Ray Stannard; Steffens, Lincoln; Tarbell, Ida M.

Mugwumps, **10E:359; 11**:913

Muir, John, **9E:319,** *319*

Mullan, John, **9**:734, **9E:319–20**

Munich Olympics, **17E:619**

Munich Pact, **15E**:524–25

Murrieta, Joaquin, **6E:209**

Murrow, Edward R. **16E:578–79,** *578*

Muscovy Company, **1**:66

Music

  blues, **12E**:420

  see also individual composers and lyricists

Musical, Broadway, **16**:*1396–97*

Muskie, Edmund Sixtus, **17E:619–20,** *619*

Mussolini, Benito, **15**:1265, *1267,* 1297, 1305, **15E:540**

MX missile system, **18**:1545

My Lai massacre, **17**:1447, 1449

N

NAACP (National Association for the Advancement of Colored People), **15E**:527, 528; **17E**:600

Nader, Ralph, **17E:620,** *620*

Nagasaki, **15E**:538

Nahuatl, **1E**:4

Napoleon Bonaparte, **4**:335–36, 344, 347, **4E:136–37,** *136*

Napoleonic Wars, **4**:338

Narraganset Indians, **2E**:66

Narvaez, Panfilo de, **1**:83, **1E:24–25**

NASA (National Aeronautics and Space Administration), **16E**:587–88; **17**:1500, 1517, **17E:596–97**

Nasser, Gamal Abdel, **17**:1451

Nation, Carrie, **11**:946, **11E:391**

National Academy of Sciences, **10**:818

National Association for the Advancement of Colored People (NAACP), **15E**:527, 528; **17E**:600

National Association of Manufacturers, **12**:1053

National bank, **4**:306, 309

  see also Bank of the United States

National character, **1**:9

National Civic Federation, **12**:1052, 1053

National Credit Association, **14**:1178

National debt

  in post revolutionary era, **4**:304–6

  see also Deficit, federal budget

National Farmers' Alliance, **10**:854–56, **10E:359–60**

National Farm Workers Association, **17E**:599

National Grange of the Patrons of Husbandry, *see* Granges

National Industrial Recovery Act (NIRA), **14**:1186, 1242, 1253–54

Nationalism, **13**:1152

  in early 1800's, **5**:367–68, 370, 374

National Labor Relations Act (NLRA), **14**:1257; **16**:1358–59

National Labor Relations Board (NLRB), **14**:1247

National Lawyers Guild, **13E**:478

National Organization for Women (NOW), **17E:622–23**

National Recovery Administration (NRA), **14**:*1185,* 1186, 1241

National Republican Party (Whig Party), **5**:401

National Road (Cumberland Road), **5**:430–31, **5E**:161

National Woman Suffrage Association, **11**:946, **11E:391–92,**
Native Americans, *see* Indians
NATO (North Atlantic Treaty Organization), **16**:1362, 1385, **16E:579**
Naturalization and Alien Acts, **4**:314, 316, **4E:137**
Nautilus, U.S.S., **16E:592**
Navahos, **9**:797
Navigation, **1**:17, **1E:25**
  gyroscope and gyrocompass, **12E:437**
Navigation Acts, **2**:151–52, **2E:43, 62**
Navy, U.S., **5E:161–62**; **8E:274**; **15**:1268, 1271
  American Revolution and, **3**:222, *222–23,* 226, **3E:79,** 93–94
  Civil War and, **8**:685, *685–96*
  Great White Fleet, **12E:419–20**
  Jefferson and, **4**:333–34
  in War of 1812, **4**:346–47
  in World War II, **15**:1291–92
Nazi Germany, **14**:1218, 1226; **15**:1265
  Holocaust, **16E:570**
  Nuremberg trials, **15E:534–35,** *535*
  in World War II, **15**:1268, 1270–73, 1291–92, **1301–5,** 1296–97, **15E:532–33**
Neagle, John, **5E:174**
Nebraska, **7**:*555*
"Necessary and proper" clause, **18**:1594
Negro troops, **8E:287,** *287*
Neighborhood Youth Corps, **16**:1426
Nelson, Horatio, **4E:137,** *137*
Netherlands, the, *see* Holland
Neutrality Act (1939), **15**:1267, 1273
Nevada, **9**:725
  gold in, **9:730–32**
Nevins, Allen, **1**:8–9; **13**:1163–68, *1167*
New Amsterdam, **1**:47, **1E:25,** *25;* **2**:*103* (map)
New Brunswick, **2E:40; 6E:189**
New Deal, **10**:860; **14**:1185–87, **1239–50**
  evaluation of, **14**:1249–50
  Second, **14:1242–44**
  see also Roosevelt, Franklin Delano
New England
  colonial, **1**:76, **1E:33; 2**:95–99
  Embargo Act and, **4**:340–41
  secession and, **4**:349
  textile mills in, **5**:*378–81,* 425–28, *429*
New England Company (later Massachusetts Bay Company), **2**:95–96, **2E:72**
New England Confederation, **3**:252, 253
New Federalism, **18**:1561
New Foundland, **1**:71, 76
New France, **1:43–47, 1E:5**
New Freedom, **13**:1121
New Guinea, **15**:1298, *1298,* 1300
New Hampshire, **2**:97; **3E:77,** 89
New Harmony, **6E:209,** *209*

New Haven Colony, *see* Eaton, Theophilus
New immigration, **10E:360,** *360*
New Jersey, **2**:100, **2E:43; 3**:250
  colonial, **2**:103
New Jersey Plan, **4**:285, 286, *287,* **4E:137–38**
Newman, Barnett, **16**:*1370–71*
New Netherland, **1**:48; **1E:25** (map); **2**:99, 100, 102, *103* (map)
  see also New Amsterdam; Stuyvesant, Petrus
New Orleans, **6**:460; **7**:*584*
  Battle of, **4**:345, *349,* **4E:138**
Newport Tower, **1E:25–26,** *25*
Newspapers, **13**:1158–59
  in colonial America, **2E:74**
  Cuba and (19th century), **12**:998–99, 1004–6
  late 19th century, **11**:937–39, **11E:375,** 395–96
  yellow journalism, **11E:395–96**
  see also individual publishers and newspapers; Muckrakers
New Sweden, **1E:26**
New York, **2**:100; **3E:77,** 89
  colonial, **2**:102–3, *103*
  Erie Canal and, **5**:*432–33,* 433–34
  trade and, **4**:280
  see also New Netherland
New York Central Railroad, **10**:836, **10E:369**
New York City, **11**:*920;* **12**:*1037–40, 1045;* **14**:1218–19; **18**:1538–39
  Brooklyn Bridge, **11**:934; **12**:*1038–39,* **12E:432**
  Central Park, **11**:*920,* **11E:394**
  Empire State Building, **14E:493,** *493*
  late 19th century, **11**:*930,* **932–37,** *932–33*
  Manhattan, **4**:336
    purchase of, **1E:22**
  political bosses, **11**:913–14, **11E:402**
  see also New Amsterdam
New York School, The, **16**:1365
New York Sun, **11E:379–80**
New York Times, **11E:393**
New York Weekly Journal, **2E:74**
New York World's Fair (1939), **14**:*1225,* 1226
Nez Perce, **9**:798–99, **9E:315**
Nicaragua, **12**:1035; **14**:1216; **18**:1545–46, 1569, **18E:657–58**
Nicolet, Jean, **1E:26**
Nicolls, Capt. Richard, **1E:25**
Niebuhr, Reinhold, **14**:1222
Nimitz, Adm. Chester W., **15**:1294, 1300, 1305, *1307,* **15E:540–41**
Nia, **1**:11, 24
Nineteenth Amendment, **11**:946
NIRA (National Industrial Recovery Act), **14**:1186, 1242, 1253–54
Nixon, Richard M., **1**:6; **16**:1416; **17**:1458, *1472,* **1473–84,** *1473, 1479,* **17E:621–22,** *621;* **18**:1535
  China and, **17:1478**

Nixon, Richard M. (*cont.*)
  domestic policies, **17**:1477
  impeachment and resignation, **17**:1484
  1972 election, 1478–80
  Vietnam policy, **17:1474–75,** 1478–79
  Watergate scandal, **17:1480–81, 1483–84,**
    1519–28, 17E:628–29
Niza, Marcos de, **1**:39, **1E:26,** 26
NLRA (National Labor Relations Act), **14**:1257;
  16:1358–59
NLRB (National Labor Relations Board), **14**:1247
Noland, Kenneth, **16**:*1372*
Nomura, Kichisaburo, **15**:*1273,* 1274
Non-Importation Act, **4**:339, **4E:138**
Non-Intercourse Act, **4**:341, 344, **4E:138**
Norris, Benjamin Franklin (Frank), **11**:967, 970,
  11E:392–93, *392*
Norsemen, *see* Vikings
North, Frederick, **3E:100,** *100*
North, Lord, **2**:164, 168; **3**:185, 186, 226; **4**:338
North, Lt. Col. Oliver, **18**:1574, *1574*
North Atlantic Treaty Organization (NATO),
  16:1362, 1385, **16E:579**
North Carolina, **2**:100–2, **2E:46**; **3**:250
Northern (or Northwestern) Alliance (National
  Farmers' Alliance), **10E:359–60**
Northern Pacific Railroad, **9**:776, **805–8; 10**:821,
  849–50, 872
North Korea, **16**:1387
  see also Korean War
North Vietnam, **16**:1390; **18**:1536
Northwest Conspiracy, **8E:288**
Northwest Ordinance of 1787, **4:285, 4E:138;**
  5:376; **6**:465
Northwest Passage, **1E:6**
Northwest Territory, **4E:**119, 138; **5**:370
  Indians and, **4E:**132, **145**
Nova Scotia, **2**:*153,* **2E:40**
Novels, *see* Literature
NOW (National Organization for Women),
  17E:622–23, *623*
Nowell, Increase, **2E:62**
Noyes, John Humphrey, **6E:209–10**
NRA (National Recovery Administration),
  14:*1185,* 1186, 1241, 1247
Nuclear energy, **18**:1542
  Atomic Energy Commission (AEC), **15E:538;**
    16E:580–81
  Three-Mile Island accident, **17**:1515–16,
    1515
Nuclear weapons, **15E:551; 18**:1545
  testing of, **16E:579–80**
  see also Atomic bomb
Nungesser, Charles, **13**:*1116*
Nuremberg trials, **15E:534–35,** *535*
Nye, Gerald P., **14**:1220, **14E:506**
Nye Committee, **14**:1220, 1221

O

Oakley, Annie, **11E:393,** *393*
Oberlin College, **6**:493
Ochs, Adolph Simon, **11E:393**
O'Connor, Sandra Day, **18**:1575, **18E:658–59,** *658*
Odets, Clifford, **14**:1222
Office of Price Administration (OPA), **15**:1337–38
Oglethorpe, James Edward, **2**:105, *106,* **2E:62**
O. Henry, **12E:429,** *429*
Ohio Valley, **2**:132
Oil industry, **10**:816–17, *817,* 871, **10E:345–46,** 365
Ojeda, Alonso de, **1E:26,** 26
O'Keeffe, Georgia, **14**:*1228*
Oklahoma Land Rush, **9E:320**
Old-Age Revolving Pension, **14**:1220, **14E:513**
Old-Man-Afraid-of-His-Horses, **9**:792
Old Northwest, **4E:119**
O'Leary, Mrs. Patrick, **9E:305**
Olive Branch Petition, **3**:190, *192,* **3E:100**
Olmsted, Frederick Law, **11E:393–94,** *394*
Olney, Richard, **12**:996, 997, **12E:429–30**
Omaha Beach, **15**:1280–81, 1286–87, 1302
Oñate, Juan de, **1E:26–27**
Oneida Community, **6E:210**
O'Neill, Eugene, **15E:541,** *541*
O'Neill, Thomas Phillip, **18E:659**
One-Tenth Plan (Lincoln Plan), **8**:700
Ontario, Lake, **1E:5**
OPA (Office of Price Administration), **15**:1337–38
OPEC (Organization of Petroleum Exporting
  Countries), **17E:623; 18**:1542
Open-door policy, **12**:*1028–29,* 1032
Oppenheimer, Julius Robert, **16E:580–81,** *580*
Optic, Oliver, **11E:394**
Ordinance of 1785, **4**:285, **4E:138–39,** *139* (map);
  6:456; **10**:845
Ordinance of Nullification, **5**:*399,* 399–400,
  5E:174–75
Oregon, **5**:366; **6**:515, **517–18,** 521–22; **9**:725, 730
Oregon Trail, **6**:518, 524, **6E:210–11**
Oregon Trunk, **9**:808
Organization of American States (OAS), **12E:431**
Original Package Case (*Brown vs. Maryland*),
  5:373, **5E:156**
Oriskany, Battle of, **3E:80, 91,** 104–5
Orlando, Vittorio, **13**:1100, 1101, *1103,* **13E:469,**
  469
Orme, Capt. Robert, **2**:*110*
Osgood, Samuel, **4E:139**
Ostend Manifesto, **7E:247**
O'Sullivan, John Louis, **6E:211**
Oswald, Lee Harvey, **16**:1424; **17E:627**
Otis, Harrison Gray, **4E:139–40**
Otis, James, **2E:62–63,** *62*; **3E:108**
Outer Mongolia, **15**:1333

Outlaws
  train robbers, **10:**839
  in the West, **9E:**300–1
    cattle drives, **9:***751–53*
  women, **9E:**301–2, 330
  see also Pirates
Overland Trail, **6:**525
  see also Oregon Trail
Overproduction, **10:**850–51
Oviedo, Lope de, **1:**84
Owen, Robert, **6E:***209, 211*

P

Pacific Doctrine, **18:**1539
Pacific Fur Company, **6:**514, **6E:**190
Pacific Ocean, **1E:**4
Pacific Railway Acts, **10:**833, **10E:**360–61
Packers and Stockyards Act (1921), **13:**1130
PACs (political action committees), **18E:659–60**
Page, Thomas Nelson, **11:**970–71, **11E:394–95**
Page, Walter Hines, **13:**1086, 1090, **13E:469–70**
Pageot, Alphonse, **5:**405
Pahlavi, Shah Mohammad Reza, **18:**1551
Paine, Robert Treat, **3E:100**
Paine, Thomas, **3:**189, 190, *199,* 199, **3E:100–1,** *101*
Painting, *see* Art
Pakenham, Sir Edward Michael, **4:**348, *349,* **4E:140**
Palestinian Liberation Organization (PLO),
    18:1552, 1564, **18E:**659
Palmer, Alexander Mitchell, **13:**1155, **13E:470**
Palmer, Nathaniel, **5E:175**
Palmer, William Jackson, **9:**776, **9E:**320, *320*
Palmer Raids, **13E:470**
Panama, **1E:**4; **12:**1026
Panama Canal, **6E:**197–98; **12:***1024,* 1025–26,
    12E:411–12, **430**
Panama Canal Treaty, **18:***1543,* 1544
Panama Canal Zone, **14:**1216–17
Pan-American Union, **12:**996, **12E:430–31**
Panay incident, **14E:506–7,** *506*
Panic of 1819, **5E:175**
Panic of 1837, **5E:175,** **6:**518
Panic of 1857, **9E:320–21,** *321*
Panic of 1873, **10:**828, 847, **10E:361**
Panic of 1883, **10E:361**
Panic of 1893, **10E:361,** *361*
Paraguay, **1E:**5
Paris, **1:**14
Paris, Treaty of (1763), **2:**125
Paris, Treaty of (1783), **3E:107;** **4:**281
Parker, Alton Brooks, **10:**897; **12E:431**
Parker, Ely S., **9E:**303
Parker, Isaac Charles, **9E:**321
Parker, Sir Peter, **3E:101**
Parker, Quanah, **9:**797

Parker, Theodore, **6E:211**
Parks, Rosa, **16E:**562
Parrington, Vernon Louis, **11E:395**
Paterson, William, **4:***287,* **4E:140**
Patronage, **10:**875
Patrons of Husbandry, *see* Granges
Patterson, John Henry, **12E:431**
Patton, Gen. George S., Jr., **15:**1296, 1302,
    15E:541–42, *542*
Pauperism, **6:**488, 490
Pawnee Indians, **6:***514–15*
Peabody, George, **5E:175–76,** *176*
Peace Corps, **16E:**581
Peace of Ghent, **4:**348–49, **4E:140**
Peace of Ryswick (1697), **2:**126, **2E:**63
Peale, Charles Wilson, **4:***350,* 351–58, *352–53, 357,*
    4E:140–41, *140*
Pearl Harbor, **15:**1291–92
Pemberton, Gen. John, **8:**654
Pendergast, Tom, **15E:**549
Pendleton, George Hune, **10:**878, **10E:**362, *362*
Pendleton Act (1883), **10:**878, **10E:362**
Penn, William, **2:**103–5, *104,* **2E:**63, *63*
Pennsylvania, **3:**248, 254
  colonial, **2:**100, 104–5, 108, **2E:**63
  constitution of, **3:**246–47
Pennsylvania Railroad, **10:**828
Pentagon Papers, The, **17:**1476, **17E:623–24,** *624*
People's Party, **10E:362–63**
  see also Populists
People United to Save Humanity (P.U.S.H.),
    18E:654–55
Pequot Indians, **2:**97, 98, **2E:63–64,** *64*
Peralta Land Fraud, **9E:321–22,** *321* (map)
Perkins, Frances, **14E:507,** *507*
Perry, Matthew Calbraith, **6E:211–12,** *212*
Perry, Oliver Hazard, **4:***328–29, 332,* 346–47,
    4E:141
Pershing, Gen. John J., **9E:**302; **13:**1093, *1093,*
    13E:470–71, *470*; **15E:**538
Perth Visas, 9
Perth Assembly, **1:**58
Peru, **1:**39, **1E:**3
Peshtigo Fire, **9E:322,** *322*
Pesticides, **16E:**561
Philadelphia
  American Revolution and, **3:**214, 219, 220
  colonial, **2:***142–43;* **3:***198–99,* 214
Philadelphia Centennial Exposition of 1876, **10:**818
Philip II, King of Spain, **1:***65,* **1E:**8
Philippines, the, **12E:**410; **18E:633–34**
  Spanish-American War and, **12:**1006–7, 1009,
    1011–12
  in World War II, **15:**1291–92, 1298, 1306–9,
    15E:536–37
Phillips, Wendell, **6:**491
Phips, William, **2E:**66, 67
Phonograph, **10:**818, *823*

Photography, **10E:**347

Phyfe, Duncan, **5E:176,** *176*

Physics, **15E:**528, 529

Pickering, Timothy, **4E:141**

Pickett, Bill, **9E:322–23**

Pickett, George, **8:**648, 654, **8E:288**

Piedmonters, **2:**123

Pierce, E. D., **9:**733

Pierce, Franklin, **7:**554, 556, **7E:247**

Pike, Zebulon Montgomery, **6E:212**

Pikes Peak Hoax, **9E:323**

Pilgrims, **1:**76–77, *76–77,* 79, 80, **1E:27;** **2:**95–97,
    138, **171–74,** *175*

    Europe at the time of, **1:***49–59*

    peace treaty with American Indians (1621),
        1E:22

    see also Puritans

Pinchney, Charles Cotesworth, **4E:141**

Pinkerton, Allan, **9E:323**

Pinkerton detectives, **10:**829

Pinta, **1:**11

Pioneering spirit, **9:728–30**

Pirates

    Jean Laffite, **4E:130–31**

    see also Barbary Wars

Pitcairn, John, **3E:101**

Pitt, William, **2:**161, **2E:64;** **3:**190

Pizarro, Francisco, **1:***21,* 34, 39, **1E:27,** *27*

Placer mines, **9E:324,** *324*

Plains Indians, **6:***497–509,* 525–27, **6E:212–13,** *213*

Plantations, colonial, **2:***148–49*

Platt, Orville Hitchcock, **10:**826; **12E:431**

Pledge of Allegiance, **9E:324**

Plessy vs. Ferguson, **10E:363**

Pluto, **14:**1210–11

Plymouth, England, **2:***172*

Plymouth Colony, **1:**54, 79–80, *80–81;* **2:**95, 171,
    173

Plymouth Company, **1:**67, 73

Plymouth Rock, **1E:27**

Pocahontas, **1E:27–28,** *28, 33*

Poe, Edgar Allan, **7E:247–48,** *248*

Poinsett, Joel, **6E:213**

Poland, **15:**1266, 1334

Political action committees (PACs), **18E:659–60**

Political parties, **4:**309; **5E:176–77**

    bosses and political machines, **11:913–14**

    origin of, in U.S., **4:**290

    social class and, **4:**309

    two-party system, **4:**290

    see also Corruption, political; *specific parties*

Polk, James K., **6:520–22,** **6E:213–14;** **7:**545, **546,**
    549

Pollack, Jackson, **16:***1366*

Polo, Marco, **1:***12–13,* **1E:28,** *28*

Ponce de León, Juan, **1:**38, **1E:28–29**

Pontiac, **2E:64**

Pontiac's Rebellion, **3E:80**

Pony Express, **324–25**

Poor Richard's Almanac, **3E:**79, 87

Pop Art, **16:**1365

Pope, John, **8:**644, 645, **8E:288–89**

Popham, Sir John, **1:***75,* 76, **1E:29**

Popular Party, **3:**194

Population

    1815, **5:**367

    1819, **5:**375

    1850, **5:**423

    1860, **6:**455

    colonial, **2:**95–96

    post-revolutionary, **4:**276

Populists (Populist Party), **10:855–60,** 875, 893,
    894, 896

    See also People's Party

Porter, Rear Adm. David Dixon, **8:**649, **8E:289**

Porter, Gen. Fitz-John, **8:644–45,** **8E:289**

Porter, Peter Buell, **5E:177**

Porter, William Sydney, *see* O. Henry

Portland & Seattle Railroad, **9:807–8**

Portugal, **1:**11, 12, 18–20

    Catholic Church's Line of Demarcation, **1E:21,**
        21 (map)

Post, Wiley, **14:**1212, *1213,* **14E:507–8**

Potawatomi Indians, **4:**346

Potsdam Conference (1945), **15:**1335, *1335,*
    15E:542

Powell, Adam Clayton, **16E:581–82**

Powell, Capt. J. W., **9E:311**

Powell vs. McCormack, **16E:592**

Powell vs. Alabama (First Scottsboro Case),
    14:1216

Powers, Francis Gary, **16:**1417

Powhatan, **1:***74,* 74, **1E:29**

Prairie Schooner, **9E:325**

Preble, Edward, **4E:141,** *141*

Preemption Act of 1830, **6E:214**

Preemption Act of 1841, *see* Distribution-Preemp-
    tion Act of 1841

Prescott, Samuel, **3:**185, **3E:101**

President, the

    election of, **4:**287–88

    Constitution and, **18:**1592

    Twentieth Amendment and, **14E:514**

Press, the, *see* Newspapers

Prevost, Sir George, **4E:142**

Prickly Pear Creek, **9:**737

Primogeniture, **3E:102**

Princeton

    battle of, **3:***242–43*

Princeton University, **3E:**111

Printz, Johan, **1E:26**

Prisons

    Civil War and, **8:**670, *8:670,* **8E:262**

    reforms, **6E:199**

Proclamation of 1763, **2:**154

Progressive Party, **12:**1055; **13:**1124; **14E:516**

Prohibition, **10**:898; **12**:1056, *1058*, **12E:418**;
    13:1150–52, *1151, 1153, 1154,* **13E:**465;
    14:1210, 1217–18
  repealed, **14E:514**
  see also Eighteenth Amendment
Propaganda, American Revolution and, **3**:189,
    194–96, **3E:**101
Prospectors, **9**:*724, 730–32, 733*
  see also Gold
Prostitution, **12**:1056
Protestant Reformation, **1E:**8
Protestants, in colonial America, **2E:**46
Public Works Administration, **14**:*1245,* 1248
Puck, **10**:*824,* 875
Pueblo incident, **17**:1452
Pueblo Indians, **1E:**5, 29–30
Puerto Rico, **1E:**28; **12**:1009
Pulaski, Casimir, **3E:102**
Pulitzer, Joseph, **11E:395–96,** *395*
Pullman, George M., **10**:820, 830, 841, **10E:363–64,**
    364
Pullman Palace Car, **10**:*841*
Pullman strike, **10**:*828–29,* 830, **10E:364**
Puna Island (Ecuador), **1E:**7
Puritans, **1**:68–70, **1E:**19, **29**; **2**:**95–96,** 99, 100, *138,*
    171–74, 176–78
  background of, **2:174, 176–78**
  beliefs of, **2:171, 178**
Pusey, Merlo, **14**:1253–58
P.U.S.H. (People United to Save Humanity),
    18E:654–55
Putnam, Israel, **3E:102**
Pynchon, William, **2**:174, 176, **2E:64–65**

Q

Qaddafi, Muammar, **18**:1566, **18E:**656, 657
Quakers, **2**:*139,* **2E:**43, **65,** *65*
  in colonial America, **2**:103–5
Quantrill, William Clarke, **8E:289–90**
Quartering Act, **2**:155–56
Quebec, **1E:**5
  American Revolution and, **3**:209, *211*
  colonial, **1E:**7, 8
  siege of, **2**:*118–21*
Queen Anne's War (War of the Spanish Succes-
    sion), **2**:109, 127–28, **2E:65–66**
Quetzalcoatl, **1**:*28, 30,* **1E:**4, **29**
Quivira, **1E:29–30**

R

Rabaul, **15**:1298, 1300
Racial discrimination
  reverse, **18**:1549
  see also Civil rights; Segregation

Radical Republicans, **8**:*702,* 711
  Civil War and, **8**:644–45, 710
  Reconstruction and, **8:698–706**
Radio, **12**:1062; **13**:1158; **14**:1209
  in 1930s, **14**:1226
Railroads, **5**:*386–98,* **435–41,** *436–39, 441,* **5E:**177;
    9:730, 761, 766, 773, 776, *802,* **9E:**316, 320,
    328; **10**:847, **10E:**353, 358–59, 363–64,
    368–70; **11E:**376; **13**:1128
  agriculture and, **5**:441
  Credit Mobilier scandal, **10E:**343
  electric, **11**:932–33
  farming and, **9**:768, 769; **10**:849, 852–53,
    853
  golden spike, **10**:*834–35*
  Granger laws and, **10E:**352
  heyday of, **10**:*842–43*
  Hill and, **9**:**808,** **9E:**314
  immigration and, **10**:849–50, 888
  Indians and, **9**:*794–95,* 795, 799–800; **10**:*838*
  industry and, **5E:**160; **10**:816, 817, 821, 825,
    827–29, 830, *831–43*
  invention and, **10**:820–21
  land grants to, **10**:852, *853* (maps)
  mergers of, **10**:*836–37*
  Pacific Railway Acts, **10E:360–61**
  riding on, **10**:*840–41*
  robber barons and, **10**:*852–53*
  station lunch counter, **10**:*840–41*
  strikes and, **10**:*827–29,* 830
  transcontinental, **10E:360–61**
  World War I and, **13**:1096–97
Raleigh, Sir Walter, **1**:*61,* 71–73, **1E:30,** *30*
Ralston, William C., **9E:**312
Randolph, Asa Philip, **15E:543,** *543*
Randolph, Edmund, **4**:*284,* 285, 286, **4E:142;**
    18:1590–91
Randolph, John, **5E:177–78,** *177*
Raskob, John J., **14E:**485
Rauschenberg, Robert, **16**:*1379*
Rauschenbusch, Walter, **10E:**364
Rayburn, Samuel Taliaferro, **16E:582,** *582*
Reagan, Ronald Wilson, **1**:7; **18**:1540, 1546, *1559,*
    1560, **1561–75,** *1563, 1572,* **18E:660–61**
  the economy under, **18:1562–64**
  election of 1980, **18**:1552
  election of 1984, **18**:1569–70
  foreign policy, **18:1564–69,** **18E:**658
  Iran-Contra affair and, **18E:650–53**
Reavis, James Addison, **9E:**321–22
Reconstruction, **8:697–711**
  blacks and, **8**:710–11, *711*
  carpetbaggers and, **8**:706, 707, *709,* 710
  Democrats and, **8**:708–9
  failure of, **8**:710–11
  Lincoln and, **8**:698–700
  Radical Republicans and, **8**:698–706
Reconstruction Acts, **8E:290**

Reconstruction Finance Corporation (RFC), **14:**1178, 1185

Red Cloud, **9:***782,* 792, 793, **9E:325**

Red Scare (1920s), **13:**1155–56

Reed, James A., **13:**1134, **13E:471**

Reed, Thomas B., **11:**909, **11E:396**

Reed, Walter, **12E:432,** *432*

Reform movements, **6:**487–94; **10:**876–81, **943–46**
  immigration laws and, **10:886–89**
  silver vs. gold and, **10:880–81, 884–86**
  tariffs and, **10:879–80,** *881–883*
  see also individual reformers and specific
      movements

Rehnquist, William H., **18:**1575, **18E:661–62,** *661*

Religion
  in late 19th century, **10E:364; 11:914–18;**
      11E:391, 400
  in early 20th century, **12:**1056–57
  in 1930s, **14:**1222
  American Revolution and, **3:**250
  in colonial America, **2:95–99, 2E:**46, 53–54
  revivalists and evangelists, **14E:502–3,** 512–13
  Scopes trial and, **10E:366**
  see also specific religions

Religious Right, rise of the, **18E:662–63**

Remington, Frederic S., **1:***82;* **9:***727,* 752–53, 760,
      9E:325; 12:*997,* 999

Removal Act of 1830, **6E:214**

Reno, Marcus, **9E:325–26,** *326*

Repartimiento (apportionment) system, **1:**40,
      1E:30

Republican Party, U.S., **7:**557–58, 560, **8:**698–99,
      708; **10:**815, 856, 858–60, 875, 877–78, 880,
      884–85, 891, 893–94, 896
  1870s–1890s, **11:**910–13
  Half Breed, **10E:339; 11:**912
  Liberal, **10E:357**
  Radical, **8:***702,* 711
    Civil War and, **8:**644–45, 710
    Reconstruction and, **8:698–706**
  Stalwarts, **11:**912
  see also Elections

Reuther, Walter Philip, **13E:458; 16E:582–83,** *583*

Revels, Hiram Rhoades, **10E:364–65**

Revenue Act, **2:**161

Revere, Paul, **2:***160,* 162, *162;* **3:**185, *187,*
      3E:102–3, *103* (map)

Reverse discrimination, **18:**1549

Revolutionary War, *see* American Revolution

Reykjavik summit (1986), **18:**1571

Reynolds, Joseph Jones, **9:**796, **9E:326**

RFC (Reconstruction Finance Corporation),
      14:1178, 1185

Rhett, Robert Barnwell, **7E:248**

Rhineland, **15:**1266

Rhode Island, **2:**165–66, 177; **3:**252
  colonial, **2:**97–98, 156, **2E:**65

Ribaut, Jean, **1E:30–31**

Richardson, Elliott L., **17:**1481, 1483

Richardson, Henry Hobson, **9E:326–27,** *326*

Richelieu, Armand Jean du Plessis de, Cardinal,
      1E:31

Richelieu, Cardinal, **1:**43

Richmond (Virginia), Union Army's approach to,
      8:638–39, *638–39,* 642–44, *643*

Richthofen, Manfred von, **13:**1107, *1117,* **13E:471**

Rickenbacker, Edward Vernon ("Eddie"),
      13:*1117,* **13E:472**

Rickover, Hyman George, **16E:583–84**

Ridgway, Gen. Matthew B., **15E:543–44; 16:**1388

Rights of Man, The, **3E:103**

Right-to-life/pro-choice debate, the, **18E:662**

Riis, Jacob August, **11:**943; **11E:396,** *396;* **12:**1053

Rio Grande, **1E:3**

Ritchie, Albert C., **13:**1126, **13E:472**

Rittenhouse, David, **4E:142,** *142*

Roads and highways, **5:**428–32, *430, 431;*
      9E:319–20
  to the West, **6:**524

Roanoke Island, **1:**71, 72, **1E:31–32**

Robber barons, **10:825–27, 852–53,** *861–73*
  see also specific people

Robbers, train, **10:**839

Roberts, Owen J., **14:**1254, 1256, **14E:508,** *508*

Robinson, Jack Roosevelt ("Jackie"), **16E:584,** *584*

Robinson, John, **2:**171, 173

Robinson, Joseph Taylor, **14:***1257,* 1257–58,
      14E:508–9

Robots, **17:**1510

Rochambeau, Count Jean Baptiste de Vimeur de,
      3E:103–4, *104*

Rockefeller, John D., **10:**816, 869, *870–71,* 872;
      10E:365; 11:909, *952*

Rockefeller, Nelson, **16E:584; 17E:624; 18:**1535

Rockingham, Charles, **2:***158,* 159; **3E:104**

Rockwell, Norman, **15:***1264*

Rocky Mountain Fur Company, **6E:190**

Rocky Mountain News, **9:**732

Roebling, John, **7E:248–49**

Roebling, Washington Augustus, **12E:432**

Roe v. Wade, **17E:599; 18E:662**

Rogers, William P., **13E:472–73,** *472;* **17:**1478

Rolfe, John, **1E:32**

Roman Catholics, *see* Catholic Church

Roman Nose, **9:**783, *783*

Rommel, Field Marshall Erwin, **15:**1275, 1285,
      1296, **15E:544,** *544*

Roosevelt, Eleanor, **14:**1191, *1192,* 1198, **14E:509**

Roosevelt, Franklin Delano, **10:**855, 860; **13:**1121,
      13E:449; 14:1180–1207, *1181, 1192–96,*
      1199–1207, 1218, 1239, **14E:509–10; 15:***1272,*
      1338, **15E:544–45**
  assassination attempt (1933), **14:**1216
  childhood of, **14:***1188–91,* 1189, 1191
  death of, **15:**1338, *1339*
  election of 1932, **14:**1180–81

Roosevelt, Franklin Delano (*cont.*)
  fireside chats, **14:**1183, *1199*
  foreign policy, **14:**1217, 1226
  Hundred Days, **14:**1181–82
  opposition to, **14:1244–46**
  Second New Deal and, **14:1242–44**
  Supreme Court and, **14:**1245–46, **1253–58**
  World War II and, **15:1266–74**, 1291, 1296, *1332,*
    1333, 1334, 1338
  see also New Deal
Roosevelt, James, **14:**1189
Roosevelt, Sara Delano, **14:**1189, *1198*
Roosevelt, Theodore, **10:**898; **11E:**396; **12:**1007,
  1008, 1012, **1025–28**, *1027,* 1033, *1033, 1051,*
  1052, 1055, **12E:432–33; 13E:**467
Roosevelt Corollary to the Monroe Doctrine,
  12:1028, **12E:**433–34
Root, John, **12E:**412
Roping, **9:***748*
Rose, Sir John, **9E:**331
Rose, William, **6E:214**
Rosecrans, William S., **8:**647–49, *671, 672,* 671–72,
  8E:290–91
Rosenberg spy case, **16E:584–85,** *584*
Rosenman, Samuel I., **14:**1180, **14E:**486
Ross, Betsy, **3E:104**
Ross, Robert, **4:**348, **4E:142–43**
Rothko, Mark, **16:***1367*
Rough Riders, **12:**1008–9
Roundups, **9:***744–45*
Rowlandson, Mary, **2E:66**
Rowse, A. L., **2:**171–78
Rubber, **1:**21
Ruby, Jack, **16:**1424
Ruckelshaus, William D., **17:**1483
Rush, Benjamin, **3E:104; 4:**278
Rush, Richard, **5:**365, 369
Rush-Bagot Agreement, **5:**365, *367,* **5E:178**
Rusk, (David) Dean, **16E:585,** *585*
Russell, Charles, **9:***746–47;* **9E:327; 10:***847*
Russell, William H., **9E:**324
Russia
  in World War I, **13:**1085, 1094
  see also Soviet Union
Russo-Japanese War, **12:**1032–33
Rutgers, Henry, **5E:178**
Ruth, George Herman ("Babe"), **13:***1149,* 1150,
  13E:473, *473*
Rutledge, Edward, **3E:104**
Rutledge, John, **4E:143**
Rwanda, **15:**1322
Ryder, Albert Pinkham, **11:**973, **11E:396–97**

S

Saar Basin, **13E:**452
Sabin, Albert Bruce, **16E:586**

Sacagawea, **6E:214–15,** *215*
Saccacus, chief, **2E:**63–64
Sacco-Vanzetti case, **13:**1157–58, **13E:**468, **473–74,**
  474
Sadat, Anwar, **18:**1544–45
Saigon, fall of, **17E:**604
Saint-Aulaire, Felix Achille, **5E:**178–79
Saint-Gaudens, Augustus, **11:**973, **11E:397,** *397*
St. Lawrence River, **1E:**6
St. Leger, Barry, **3E:104–5**
St. Louis (Missouri), **5:***422*
St. Patrick's Day, **10:***886*
St. Paul (Minnesota), **9:**804, *804*
St. Paul, Minneapolis & Manitoba Railroad, **9:**804
St. Paul & Pacific Railroad, **9:**804
Sakhalin, **12:**1033
Salem (Massachusetts), **2:**95, *97*
  witchcraft trials, **2E:**66–67
Salk, Jonas Edward, **16E:586,** *586*
Salomon, Haym, **3E:**105
SALT (Strategic Arms Limitation Talks), **17:**1478
SALT II, **18:**1545
Salt Lake Valley (Utah), **6:**524, 525
Saltonstall, Sir Richard, **2:**174, 176, *176,* **2E:67**
Samoset, **1:**79
Sampson, Rear Adm. William T., **12:**1009, **12E:434**
Sandburg, Carl, **16E:586–87,** *586*
Sand Creek Massacre, **9E:**327
Sandinistas, **18:**1546, **18E:657–58**
Sandino, Cesar Augusto, **18E:**657
Sandys, George, **1E:**32
Sandys, Sir Edwin, **1:***49,* **1E:**32
San Francisco earthquake, **12E:434–35,** *434*
San Ildefonso, Treaty of, *see* Charles IV, King of
  Spain
San Juan Hill, Battle of, **12:***1004–5,* 1009, *1018–19*
Sankey, Ira D., **11:**918, **11E:**391
San Salvador, **1:**11
Santa Anna, Antonio Lopez de, **6:**520, *521;*
  7:*564–65, 567,* **7E:249–50**
Santa Fe Trail, **6:**524, **6E:215**
Santa Maria, **1:**11
Santee Sioux, **9:**779, **9E:**309, 316, 328–29
Sante Fe (Atchison, Topeka & Santa Fe) Railroad,
  9:776, 805
Saratoga, Battle of, **3:***216–18,* 219–20, **3E:**80, **81,**
  84, **88,** 94
Sargent, John Singer, **11:***980,* 982–84, 987,
  11E:397–98, *398*
Satank, **9E:327–28,** *327*
Satanta, **9E:**328
Saturday Night Massacre, **17:**1483, 1522
Sauk Indians, **6E:**193
Sawyer, Philetus, **11E:**398
Scalia, Antonin, **18:**1575
Scheer, George F., **3:**261–68
Schiff, Jacob H., **9:**806, **9E:**328
Schirra, Walter M., Jr., **17:***1491*

Schlesinger, Arthur, Jr., **16**:1432, 1433

Schneiderman, Rose, **12E:435**

Schools, *see* Education

Schurz, Carl, **10**:815, 877, **10E:365–66**, *366*

Schuyler, Philip John, **3E:105**

Schwab, Charles M., **12E:435**

Science, technology, and inventions, **4E**:142; **10**:818

  1940s–1980s, **17:1503–17**

  agriculture, mechanization of, **5**:*384–85*, **443–48**; **8**:700; **10**:848; **12**:1059; **13**:1131

  automated production, **17:1510**

  city life and, **11:932–37**

  computers, **17:1503–10**

  cotton gin, **5**:*378, 442,* **443–46**, **445**; **7**:582–83

  cyclotron, **14**:1215, **14E**:450, 499

  disasters, technological, **17:1514–16**

  electricity (electric power), **10E**:368; **11**:932; **12**:*1040–41,* **1060, 1062**

  electric light, **10**:818, 820, 821, **10E**:348; **12**:1060, *1064;* **13**:1128–29

  genetic engineering, **17:1512–13**

  heart transplants, **17:1513–14**

  lasers, **17:1511–12**

  naval, **8**:*688–91*

  navigation, **1E:25**

    astrolabe, **1**:17, **1E**:3

    gyroscope and gyrocompass, **12E:437**

  nuclear energy, **18**:1542

  railroads and, **10**:820–21

    air brakes, **10**:821, 849, **10E:369–70**

  religion and, **11:914–15**

  sewing machine, **5E:166–67**, **180**, *180*

  telegraph, **5E:160**, **174**; **9**:795; **10**:825, **10E**:348; **11**:*935,* **11E:381–82**

  telephone, **10**:818, *822,* 825, **10E**:338; **11**:936; **12:1062–64**, *1065*

  tinkerers and inventors, **10:818, 820–21**

  westward movement and, **10:847–49**, *848*

  see also Aviation; Communications; Evolution; Industrialization; Industrial Revolution; Space exploration; Transportation; *individual scientists and inventors*

SCLC (Southern Christian Leadership Conference), **18E:654**

Scopes trial, **10**:*897,* 897, **10E:366**

Scott, David R., **17**:1492

Scott, Dred, **7**:559, *559*

Scott, Thomas Alexander, **12E:435**

Scott, Gen. Winfield, **7**:*548,* 549, 554, *573,* **7E:249–50**; **8**:636, 637, 642

Scottsboro Boys, **14E:510–11**, *510*

Seale, Bobby, **17E:600**

Sears, Stephen W., **6**:531–38

SEATO (Southeast Asia Treaty Organization), **16**:1390, **16E:587**

Secession, **4**:349; **5**:400

  North and, **4E:127**

Second Bank of the United States, **5E:179**; **10**:852

Second Continental Congress, **3**:186, **3E:79**, 82, **83**, 91, 92

  see also Continental Congress

Sectionalism, **5**:374–76; **7**:609

  before Civil War, **7:549–60**

Sedition Act, **4**:314–15, 333, **4E:143**

  see also Alien and Sedition Acts

Segregation

  in 1950s and 1960s, **16E:561–62**

  Brown v. Board of Education case, **16**:1420; **17E**:616

  busing to end, **17E:599**

  in Little Rock (Arkansas), **16**:1420

  Montgomery (Alabama) bus boycott against, **16E**:562

  Plessy vs. Ferguson case, **10E:463**

  of schools, **16**:1420; **17E**:616

  "separate but equal" doctrine, **10E:363**

  see also Blacks; Civil rights; Civil Rights Act; Civil-rights movement

Selective Training and Service Act (1940), **15**:1268

  see also Draft, military

Seminole Indians, **5**:366, **5E:179–80**, *179;* **6E**:213

Senate, U.S., **18**:1591

  see also Congress, U.S.

"Separate but equal" doctrine, **10E:363**

Separation of powers, **4**:288

Separatists, **1**:49, 54, 56, 58, 61, 68–70, 76, **1E:32**, **2E**:45, 54, 71; **4**:281

  Northern, **4**:337–38

Sequoyah, **5E:180**, *180*

Serapis, **3**:224, *224–25,* **3E**:79

Serbia, **13**:1085

Settlement houses, **11**:946

Seven Cities of Cibola, **1**:39, **1E:8–9**

Seven Days' Battles, **8**:643

Seventeenth Amendment, **12E:435–36**; **18**:1591

Seven Years' War, **2**:134

Sewall, Samuel, **2E:67**

Seward, William Henry, **7**:*553,* 553–54, 609, 612, *613,* **7E:250**, *250;* **9E**:299

Seward's Folly, *see* Alaska, purchase of

Sewing machine, **5**:*180,* **5E:166–67**, **180**

Shafter, Gen. William R., **12**:*1004,* 1008, *1014–15,* **12E:436**

Share Our Wealth program, **14**:1220

Shays' Rebellion, **3E:79**; **4**:*280,* 283, **4E:143–44**

Sheeler, Charles, **14**:*1234*

Shelburne, Sir William Petty, Second Earl of, **3**:226, **3E:105**

Sheridan, Gen. Philip H., **8**:681, 683, **8E:291**; **9**:796, **9E:307**

Sherman, Roger, **4**:287, **4E:144**

Sherman, William Tecumseh, **5**:448; **8**:649, 671, 673, 676, 678–79, *679,* 683–84, 717, **8E:291–92**; **9**:*800–1,* **9E:304**

Sherman Antitrust Act, **10**:826, **10E:366–67**; **12E:414**

Sherman Silver Purchase Act, **10**:885, **10E:367** repeal of, **10**:857–58

Sherwood, Robert E., **14**:1222

Shiloh, Battle of, **8**:638, *640–41*

Shipping companies, **13**:1127–28

Shriver, R. Sargent, **17**:1480

Shultz, George Paul, **18E:663**, *663*

"Shuttle diplomacy," **18**:1539

Sibley, Col. Henry H., **9**:*779*, **9E:328–29**

Siegfried Line, **15**:1304

Silver
  Bland-Allison Act, **10E:340**
  free-silver movement, **10E:339**, 340
  gold vs., **10:880–81, 884–86**, 893–94
  mining of, **9**:731, 740
  politics and, **10:856–60**, *857*
  Populists and, **10**:856
  Sherman Silver Purchase Act, **10E:367**

Simpson, "Sockless Jerry," **10**:856, **10E:367**

Simpson, Wallis Warfield, **14**:1225

Sinclair, Henry F. (Harry), **13**:1123, **13E:475**

Sinclair, Upton Beall, **12E:436**, *436*; **14**:1220

Singer, Isaac Merritt, **5**:447, **5E:180**, *180*

"Single tax" theory, **10E:351**

Sioux Indians, **6**:*498–99, 502–3, 505*, 526–27; **9**:779, 791, 792, 796, **6E:302**, 304, 307–9, 310–11, 316, 325, 328–30

Sirica, John, **17E:628**

Sitting Bull, **9**:777, *785*, 788, 792, 796, **9E:329–30**, *329*

Skylab, **17**:1500

Slack, John, **9E:312**

Slater, Samuel, **5**:*388*, **5E:180**; **10**:818

Slavery, **3**:254, **3E:87**, *88*, 98, **4**:276, 281, 287, **4E:130**, **5**:366, 392, **5E:161–62**, *182*; **7**:*580, 582, 583*, 583, 585, 612, 614, **7E:250–51**, *250*; **8**:698
  abolitionist movement and, **6:491–93, 6E:188**, *188*, 193, 199, 203, 207; **7:554–57**, 587–88; **9E:300**
  American Revolution and, **3**:250–52
  Civil War and, **8**:671, 718
  in colonial America, **2E:65**, 67
  Compromise of 1850 and, **7**:*552*, 552–54, 626–28, **7E:231–32**
  Constitution and, **18**:1591–92
  cotton and, **5**:445
  Crittenden Compromise and, **7E:233**
  Democratic Party and, **7**:588, 609
  Dred Scott case, **5**:*422*; **7**:559–60, **7E:237**
  Emancipation Proclamation, **8**:*660*, **8E:271–72**
  freeing of, **8**:701, 702
  Freeport Doctrine and, **7E:238**
  Fugitive Slave Law, **7E:238–39**
  Indians and, **2E:63**
  Kansas-Nebraska Act and, **7E:242–43**

Slavery (*cont.*)
  Missouri Compromise and, **5**:375–76
  sectionalism and issue of, **7:550–60**
  slave trade, **1**:70; **2E:70**
  Southern justification of, **7:586–88**
  three-fifths compromise, **18**:1591–92
  underground railroad, **7E:256–57**
  Wilmot Proviso and, **7**:550, **7E:258–59**

Slidell, John, **7**:545, **7E:251**

Sloat, John D., **7**:*568*, **7E:251**

Slums, late 19th century, **11**:943, *944–45*, 945, **11E:396**

Smallwood, William, **3E:105**

Smith, Alfred E., **13**:1126, *1126*, **13E:474–75**; **14**:1244

Smith, Deaf, **7**:564

Smith, Donald, **9**:804

Smith, Jedediah S., **6:531–38**, **6E:215**

Smith, John, **1**:*73*, 74–76, **1E:27–28**, 29, **32–33**, *33*

Smith, Joseph, **6E:215–16**

Smith, Margaret Bayard, **5E:180–81**

Smith, Moe, **13E:465**

Smith, Samuel Francis, **6E:216**

Smith, Walter Bedell, **15E:545–46**

Smith Act of 1940, **13E:453**; **14E:484–85**

Smithsonian Institution, **6E:216**

Smoking, Surgeon General's report on, **17E:625**

Smoky Hill Passage, **6**:524

Smoot-Hawley Tariff, **13**:1127

Smuggling, in colonial America, **2**:155

Smyth, John, **2**:171

SNCC (Student Non-Violent Coordinating Committee), **17E:598**

Social class(es)
  late 19th-early 20th century, **12:1049–53**
  American Revolution and, **3**:193–94, 247–50
  political parties and, **4**:309

Social Darwinism, **11:960–61**, **11E:382**

Social gospel, **10E:364**

Socialism, **10**:825, **10E:344–45**
  Christian, **10E:364**; **11E:399**

Social Security Act, **14**:1243

Soil Conservation and Domestic Allotment Act (1936), **14**:1240

Somoza Debayle, Anastasio, **18**:1545, **18E:657**

Somoza Garcia, Anastasio, **18E:657**

Sons of Liberty, **2**:156, **2E:67**

Sorenson, Theodore, **16**:1432, 1433

Soulé, Pierre, **7E:247**

Sound barrier, **16E:587**

Sousa, John Philip, **12E:436–37**, *437*

South, the, **7:581–88**
  1860 election and, **7:609–12**, 615
  American Revolution and, **3**:210–11, 261–68, *262*, **3E:96**
  colonial, **2**:137, *146, 148–49*
  Confederate States of America, **7E:232**
  cotton and, **5**:370, 445; **7:582–86**

South, the (*cont.*)
  cotton gin and, **5:**443
  Dixiecrats, **16:**1364
  industrialization and, **5:***442,* 443–46, 448
  Andrew Jackson and, **5:**398–400
  Mason and Dixon Line, **7E:246**
  national government and, **3:**254
  plantations, **7:**581–84
  in post-revolutionary era, **4:**279
  secession, **7:**611, 612, 615–16, **7E:**248
  sectionalism and, **5:**374; **7:549–60**
  slavery and, **4:**281; **5:**376; **6:**492
  see also Civil War; Reconstruction; *specific*
    states
South Africa, apartheid in, **18E:663–64**
South America, *see* Latin America
South Carolina, **3:**249
  American Revolution and, **3:**210–11, *212–13,*
    261–68, *262,* **3E:**106, **107**
  colonial, **2:**100–1, 128
  constitution of, **3:**247–48
  secession, **7:**615, **7E:**248
  states' rights and, **5:**398–400, *399*
South Dakota, gold in, **9:**738–39
South East Asia Treaty Organization (SEATO),
  16:1390, **16E:587**
Southern Christian Leadership Conference
  (SCLC), **18E:654**
Southern Pacific Railroad, **9:**806, **10:**821, 872
South Korea, **16:**1387
South Vietnam, **18:**1536
  see also Vietnam War
Soviet Union, **13:**1134; **16:**1385, 1392–93; **18E:**645
  in 1960s, **16:**1417–20
  Brezhnev, Leonid, **18:**1539, 1545, **18E:636–37**
  Carter administration and, **18:**1545
  detente with, **18:**1539
  Gorbachev, Mikhail, **18:**1571, *1573,* **18E:645**
  Khrushchev, Nikita S., **16:**1392, 1417, *1435*
  Reagan administration and, **18:1570–73**
  recognized by the U.S., **14:**1217
  space flights, **17:***1486–87,* 1500, *1501,* **17E:**597
  Stalin, Joseph V., **15:**1266, *1332,* 1333, 1335,
    15E:546–47; **16:**1356, 1357, *1357,* 1392
  Vietnam War and, **17:**1450–51
  in World War II, **15:**1266, 1270, 1271, 1292–93,
    1304
  after World War II, **16:**1356–57
  see also Cold War; Russia
Soyer, Isaac, **14:***1183*
Space exploration, **16:**1417, **16E:587–88,** **17:***1479,*
  1485–1501; **18:**1539
  Apollo program, **17:***1494–1500,* 1503, 1507,
    17E:596–97, *597*
  Gemini program, **17:***1492–93,* **17E:**596–97
  Soviet, **17:***1486–87,* 1500, *1501,* **17E:**597
  space-shuttle program, **17:**1500, *1501;*
    18:1573–74

Space Exploration (*cont.*)
  Viking probes, **17:**1500
  see also individual astronauts
Spain
  American Revolution and, **3:**195, 196, 221
  conquistadors, **1:**22, 23, *29–33,* 37–39, **1E:**27
  Cuban revolts against, **12:**997–98
  England and, **2:**124–25, 127–28, 130–31
  Monroe Doctrine and, **5:**368–70
  the West and, **2:**124
  see also Spanish colonies
Spanish-American War, **12:1006–12,** *1013–23,*
  1028–29; **13E:**471
Spanish Armada, **1E:33**
Spanish Civil War, **14:**1225; **15E:**531
Spanish colonies, **1:40–43,** 48, 64, 70; **2:**100, 105–6,
  124–25, 127–28, 130–31; **5:**366, 368
  Indians in, **1:**40, **1E:**30
  Line of Demarcation, **1E:**21, *21* (map)
  Louisiana and, **4:**335
  in South America, **5:**368
  viceroys, **1:**42–43
  see also specific colonies
Spanish Succession, War of the, *see* Queen Anne's
  War
Specialization, **10:**822
Specie Circular, **5:**397, **5E:181**
Speicher, Eugene, **14:***1231*
Spencer, Herbert, **11:**959
Sperry, Elmer Ambrose, **12E:437**
Spirit of the Frontier, The (Gast), **9:***800–1*
Spoils system, **5:**393, **5E:181**, **10:**875, *876,* 877
Sports
  in 1920s, **13:**1149–50
  baseball, **11:***936, 937,* 939–40, **11E:**381; **18E:**632
  boxing, **11E:**399–400
  football, **13E:**460
  see also individual athletes
Spotsylvania, **8:**676–77
Sprague, Adm. C.A.F., **15:**1308
Spring-Rice, Sir Cecil, **13:**1085
Spruance, Adm. Raymond A., **15:**1294, 1309,
  15E:546
Sputniks, **17:**1487
Squanto, **1:**79, **1E:**22
Stadford, Leland, **11:**918
Stagecoaches, **5:**431, *430;* **9E:**332–33, *332*
Stalin, Joseph V., **15:**1266, *1332,* 1333, 1335,
  15E:546–47; **16:**1356, 1357, *1357,* 1392
Stalwart Republicans, **11:**912
Stamp Act (1765), **2:***154,* 155, 156, *157,* 158–59,
  161, **2E:67–68,** *67, 68;* **3E:**89
Stamp Act Congress, **3E:**86
Standard Oil Company of Ohio, **10:**816, 826
Standard Oil of New Jersey, **10E:**365
Standard Oil Trust, **10:**817
Standish, Miles, **2:**96, 173, **2E:**32, 68
Stanford, Leland, **10:***834–35*

Stanley, Henry Morton, **11E:398–99**

Stanton, Edwin McMasters, 8:684, *702,* 705, **8E:292**

Stanton, Elizabeth Cady, 6:491, **6E:216;** 9E:300; **11E:392**

Stark, John, **3E:105–6**

Starr, Belle, **9E:330**

Star Spangled Banner, The, 4:*330–31,* 348, **4E:144**

START (Strategic Arms Reduction Talks), **18E:650**

Star Wars, *see* Strategic Defense Initiative

State governments
  under Articles of Confederation, **4:278–85**
  constitutions, 3:245–48
  in revolutionary era, **3:245–52**

States' rights, **4:315–16; 5:370–74**
  the South and, 5:398, *399*
  Supreme Court and, **5E:164,** 182

Statue of Liberty, **10E:357, 367–68,** *368;* 18:1575–76, *1577, 1580–81, 1584*

Steamboats, **4E:124–25;** 5:*382–83,* 407, *413–19,* **5E:181;** 9:729, *729,* 804, 9E:316, 330–31, *330*

Steel industry, 10:816, *820,* **821–25, 10E:349–50**
  strikes in, 10:829–30, 867
  mills, 5:*388–89*

Steffens, Lincoln, **12E:437–38**

Steinbeck, John, **14:1219**

Stella, Joseph, 14:*1229*

Stennis, John, **17:1521–22**

Stephen, George, 9:804

Stephens, Alexander H., 7:612, *614, 615,* **7E:251–52**

Stephens, Uriah Smith, **10E:368**

Stettinius, Edward Reilley, **15E:547**

Steuben, Baron Friedrich Wilhelm von, **3E:106,** *106*

Stevens, John F., 9:808

Stevens, Thaddeus, 8:702, *702, 705,* **8E:292**

Stevenson, Adlai E., 16:1389, *1393,* 1394, 1418, **16E:588–89**

Still, Clyfford, 16:*1369*

Stilwell, Joseph Warren, **15E:547–48,** *548*

Stimson, Henry L., 14:1211; 15:1265, **15E:511**

Stockman, David Alan, 18:*1562,* **18E:664–65**

Stock market
  in 1920s, **13:1147–48**
  collapse (1987), 18:1575, **18E:665–66**
  crash of 1929, 14:1175–76, **14E:485**

Stockton, Robert F., 6:523 **6E:216–17,** *216;* 7:*568*

Stone, Harlan Fiske, 14:1254, 1256, **14E:511–12,** *512*

Stone, Lucy, **11E:392**

Stone, Samuel, 2:176, 177, **2E:68**

Stowe, Harriet Beecher, 7:555, **7E:252,** *252,*

Straight, Willard D., 12:1035, **12E:438**

Strategic Arms Limitation Talks (SALT), 17:1478, **17E:624–25**

Strategic Arms Reduction Talks (START), **18E:650**

Strategic Defense Initiative (SDI, Star Wars), 18:1571, **18E:650**

Strikes, 9E:319, 323; 10:*827,* **828–30,** *828–29,* 867

Strong, Josiah, 11:961, **11E:399**

Stuart, Gilbert, **4E:144,** *144*

Stuart, James E. B. (Jeb), 8:645, 647, **8E:292–93,** *293*

Student Non-Violent Coordinating Committee (SNCC), **17E:598**

Stuyvesant, Petrus, **1E:33–34,** *34*

Sublette, William, **6E:217**

Submarines
  in World War I, 13:1088, *1088–89,* 1092
  in World War II, 15:1273

Sudetenland, 15:1266

Suez Canal, 16:1393

Suffrage, women's, 9E:*299,* 300; 11:946, **11E:391–92**

Sugar Act (1764), 2:*153,* 155, 156, **2E:68–69,** *69*

Sullivan, John, **3E:106**

Sullivan, John Lawrence, **11E:399–400,** *399*

Sullivan, Louis, 11:973, *974–75,* 976, **11E:400**

Sullivan, Mark, **13E:475**

Sultana Disaster, **9E:330–31,** *330*

Sumner, Charles, 7:558–59, *558–59,* **7E:252–53;** 9E:299

Sumner, William Graham, 11:961

Sumter, Thomas, 3:265, 267, 268, **3E:106**

Sun Dance, **6E:213,** *213*

Sunday, William Ashley ("Billy"), **14E:512–13,** *512*

Sun Yat-sen, **15E:525**

Superior, Lake, **1E:5**

Supreme Council, 13:1101

Supreme Court, U.S., 4:288, 304, **4E:143;** 9E:312; 10:826, 887
  under Burger, **17E:598**
  civil rights cases, **10E:363,** 16:1420, **16E:561;** 17E:616
  the Constitution and, 18:1597–98
  federal government and, 5:370–74
  Indians and, 5:397
  labor decisions, 12:1053; **13:1132–33**
  John Marshall and, **5:370–74,** *371–73,* 375, 397
  New Deal cases, 14:1240, 1242, **14E:508**
  states' rights and, **5E:164,**
  Reagan administration and, 18:1575
  Roosevelt's "court-packing," **14:1245–46,** 1253–58
  under Warren, **16E:592**
  see also individual justices and specific cases

Surgeon General's Report of 1964, **17E:625**

Sussex pledge, 13:1089

Sutherland, George, 14:1254, **14E:513**

Sutter, John Augustus, 6:469, *470–71,* 524, **6E:217**

Swamp Fox (Francis Marion), 3:*260,* **261–68,** *263, 265*

Sweden, 1:48
  colonies, 1E:26
Swift, Gustavus, 10:819
Syria, 17:1451

T

Tabor, H.A.W., 11:909
Taft, Robert A., 15:1270, *1271*; 16E:589, *589*
Taft, William Howard, 10:897; 12:1033–35, 1053,
    12E:438–39, *438*, 13:1096
Taft-Hartley Act of 1947, 13E:453; 16:1359,
    16E:589–90
Taiwan, 15E:525; 16:1386
Talcott, William, 9:732
Talleyrand, Charles Maurice, **4E:144–45**, *145*
Tallmadge, James, 5:375–76, **5E:181–82**
Talmage, Thomas De Witt, **11E:400**
Tammany Hall, 11:913–14, 11E:402
Taney, Roger, **5E:182**, *182*
Tarbell, Ida Minerva, **12E:439**
Tariffs, **10:879–80**, *881–883*
  of 1828, **5E:182**
  Dingley, **10E:345**
  McKinley, **10E:358**
  Morrill, **10E:359**
  Wilson-Gorman, **10E:370**
Tarleton, Banastre, 3:266–67, *267*, **3E:106–7**
Taxation, 4E:148
  Articles of Confederation and, 3:255
  in colonial America, 2:153–57
  Constitution and, 4:286–87
  Hamilton and, 4:304, 306, 307, 309
  states' rights and, 5:398–99, *399*
Taylor, Bayard, **11E:400–1**
Taylor, Edward, **2E:69**
Taylor, Zachary, 7:545–47, 549, **550–54**, *570–71*,
    7E:253, *253*
Teamsters, 17E:608–9
Teapot Dome affair, 13:1123, 1124, 1133–34,
    13E:475, 478
Technology, *see* Science, technology, and
    inventions
Tecumseh, 4:341, 344, 346, 347, **4E:145**, *145*
Teheran Conference (1943), 15:1333, *1334*,
    15E:548–49
Telegraph, **5E:160**, 174; 9:795; 10:825, 10E:348;
    11:935, 11E:381–82
Telephone, 10:818, *822*, 825, 10E:338; 11:936;
    12:1062–64, *1065*
Television, 14:1226; 16:*1410–13*
Teller, Henry, **12E:439–40**
Teller Resolution, 12E:439
Temperance movement, 6:490–91, 6E:189, 217–18,
    220–21, *221*; 11:946, 11E:391, 407; 12:1056

Temple of the Sun, **1E:34**
Tennessee Valley Authority (TVA), 13E:478;
    14:*1184*, 1185–86, 1248
Tenochtitlán, 1:*29*, 1E:4, **32–33**, *34* (map)
Tenskwatawa, 4:*341*, **4E:145**
Tenure of Office Act, **8E:293**
Tereshkova, Valentina V., 17:*1487*
Terrorism, 18:1564–66
Terry, Gen. Alfred A., 9E:308
Tesla, Nikola, 10:821, 10E:368
Tet offensive, 17:1451–53, *1468–69*, **17E:625–26**,
Texas, 1:84; 5:366–67; 6E:190–91; 7:553
  in 19th century, **6:518–20**
  Mexican War and, 7:545, *561–65*
  secession, **7:615**, 616
Textile industry, 5:*378–81*, 425–28, *429*, **5E:155–56**
  sewing machine and, 5:*180*, **5E:166–67**, 180
Tezcatlipoca, 1:*35*
Thailand, 18:1537
Thatcher, Margaret Hilda, **18E:665**, *665*
Theater, 11:940
  late 19th century, 11E:375–76
  in 1930s, 14:1222
  in 1950s, 16:*1398–99*
  Broadway musical, 16:*1396–97*
Thirteenth Amendment, **8E:293**
Thirty Years War, 1:61, 80
Thomas, George Henry, 8:637, *672*, 672–73,
    8E:293–94
Thomas, Jesse, 5:376, **5E:182**
Thomas Amendment, 5:376
Thoreau, Henry David, 6:495, **6E:218**
Three-fifths compromise, 18:1591–92
Three-Mile Island, 17:1515–16, *1515*
Thurber, Charles, **5E:183**
Thurmond, Strom, 16:1364
Tibbets, Col. Paul W., 15:1310, 15E:538
Ticonderoga, Battle of, 2:*116*
Tiffany, Charles, 9E:312
Tilden, Samuel J., **8E:294**
Tilton, Theodore, 11:916, **11E:401**
Timber and Stone Act (1878), 10:846, *846*
Timber Culture Act of 1873, 9:773–74, **9E:331**
Timucua, 1:*36*
Tinkerers and inventors, 10:818, **820–21**
  see also Science, technology, and inventions
Tippecanoe, Battle of, 4:*340*, *341*, 344
Titanic, **12E:440**
Tito, Josip Broz, 15E:548
Titov, Gherman S., 17:1486
Tobacco, 1E:19, 20, 32, **35**, *35*; 10E:346
Tocqueville, Alexis de, 3:250; **5E:183**, *183*
Tojo, Hideki, 15:1274, **15E:549**, *549*
Tompkins, Daniel D., **4E:145**
Tonkin Gulf Resolution, **17:1446–47**, 1449
Toombs, Robert A., 7:618, **7E:253–54**
Torrio, Johnny, **14E:489**

Toscanelli, Paolo, **1E:35**
Townes, Charles H., **17:**1511
Townsend, Francis E., **14:**1219–20, **14E:513,** *513*
Townsend Plan, **14E:513**
Townshend, Charles, **2:***158,* 161
Townshend Acts, **2:**161, 164–65, **2E:69**
Trade
  15th-16th century, **1:**12, 14, 16–17
  in 1920s, **13:**1127
  American Revolution and, **3E:79, 82**
  in colonial America, **2:***144*
    fur trade, **1:**43–44, *44–45;* **2:**95, 102, 125,
      129–30
    Navigation Acts, **2:**151–52, **2E:43, 62**
    slave trade, **1:**70; **2E:70**
    triangular trade, **2:**156, **2E:69, 70,** *70* (map)
    with Great Britain
      Embargo Act, **4:**340–41, *342–43,* **4E:122**
      Non-Importation Act, **4:**339, **4E:138**
      Non-Intercourse Act, **4:**341, 344, **4E:138**
      post-revolutionary era, **4:**280–81
      War of 1812 and, **4:**317
    imbalance, 20th century, **18:**1563
    interstate, **5E:164**
      federal regulation of, **5:**372–73
      transportation and, **5:**428–41
    manufacturing and, **4:**279–80
    New York and, **4:**280
    in post-revolutionary era, **4:**278–81
    with South America, **5:**392–93
    tobacco, **2:***147–49*
    Washington and, **4:**312–13
    see also Stamp Act; Sugar Act; Tariffs
Trail of Tears, **5:***396,* 398
Transcendentalism, **6:**495, **6E:195, 218–19,** *219*
Transportation, **4:**276; **6:**456–57; **9:**759
  19th century, **6:**527–28
  in 1920s, **13:**1127–28
  Conestoga wagon, **5:**431–32, **5E:159–60**
  express services, **9E:332–33**
  interstate trade and, **5:**428–41
  railroads, **5:435–41,** *436–39, 441*
  roads and highways, **5:428–32,** *430, 431;*
    9E:319–20
  to the West, **6:**524
  shipping companies, **9E:**332; **13:**1127–28
  stagecoaches, **5:**431, *430;* **9E:**332–33, *332*
  steamboats, **4E:**124–25; **5:***382–83,* 407, *413–19,*
    5E:181; **9:**729, *729,* 804, **9E:**316, 330–31, *330*
  waterways, **5:**407, *407–21*
    canals, **5:**432–35, *432–34*
  westward expansion and, **9:729–30,** *731,* 734
  see also Railroads
Transportation Act of 1920, **13:**1128
Travis, William Barret, **7E:254,** *254*
Treadway, Sophia, **9E:322**
Treaties, *see under first significant word* (e.g.,
  Paris, Treaty of)

Trenchard, General Hugh, **13:**1115
Trent, Capt. William, **2:**132
Trent Affair, **8E:294**
Trenton, Battle of, **3:**214, **3E:91,** 94, 98
Triana, Rodrigo de, **1:**11
Triangle Fire, **12E:440–41,** *440*
Triangular trade, **2:**156, **2E:69, 70,** *70* (map)
Triple Alliance (Central Powers), **13:**1085
Triple Entente, **13:**1085
Tripolitan War, **4:**334, **4E:**115–16, *116* (map), 121,
  141, 142
Trist, Nicholas, **7E:254–55**
Truman, Harry S, **1:**6; **15:**1310, 1335, 1337,
  15E:549–51, *550;* **16:**1357–60, *1363,* 1389,
  1420, **16E:579–80, 590–91,** *590*
  Korean War and, **16:**1387–88
Truman Doctrine, **15E:538; 16:**1360, **16E:591**
Trumbo, Dalton, **16E:569**
Trumbull, John, **3E:107,** *107;* **4:**352, **4E:146**
Trumbull, Lyman, **7:**612, **7E:255**
Trusts, **10:***875;* **11:**909
  see also Monopolies
Truth, Sojourner, **7E:255**
Tubman, Harriet, **7E:255–56,** *255*
Tudor, Mary, **1E:8**
Tugwell, Rexford G., **14:**1239, **14E:486**
Tunney, James Joseph ("Gene"), **13E:476–77**
Turkey, **1:**17, **1E:**29–30
Turner, Frederick Jackson, **9:**776, **9E:332**
Turner, Nat, **7:**586, **7E:256,** *256*
Tuscarora War, **2E:70–71,** *71*
Tuskegee Institute, **11E:404**
Tutu, Archbishop Desmond, **18E:664**
Twain, Mark, **11:**905, *964,* 965–67, *967,* 970,
  11E:401–2, *402*
Tweed, William Marcy ("Boss"), **11:**913–14,
  11E:402–3
Twelfth Amendment, **5E:183; 14E:513–14**
Twenty-first Amendment, **14:**1218, **14E:514,** *514*
Twenty-second Amendment, **16E:591**
Twenty-sixth Amendment, **17E:626**
Tydings, Millard E., **14:**1249, **14E:514–15,** *515*
Tyler, John, **6:**520, 621, **6E:219**
Typhoid fever (yellow fever), **12E:432**

U

U-2 incident, the, **16E:591–92**
U-boats, **13:**1088, *1088–89,* 1092
Uncle Sam, **10:***889*
Uncle Tom's Cabin, *see* Stowe, Harriet Beecher
Underground Railroad, **7:**554, **7E:256–57,** *257*
UNESCO (United Nations Educational, Scientific
  and Cultural Organization), **15:**1326
UNICEF (United Nations Children's Fund),
  15:1325

Union Pacific Railroad, **9:**776, 805, 806; **10:**821, *833–35,* 850, 872, **10E:**360–61

Unions, *see* Labor unions

Union Stockyards, **10:***819,* 819

United Automobile Workers (UAW), **14:**1224; **16E:**582–83

United Mine Workers (UMW), **12:***1054;* **14E:**500; **16E:**575–76

United Nations, **15:***1311–31;* **16:**1393–94, **16E:**560–61
  China's membership in, **17:**1478
  Korean War and, **16:**1387–88
  Security Council, **15:***1318*

United States, **4:***318–19, 322–23*

United States Steel Company, **10:**869; **14:**1225

United States Temperance Union, *see* American Temperance Union

UNIVAC computer, **17:**1505

Universal Negro Improvement Association, **13E:**459–60

Upshur, Abel, **6E:219–20**

Urey, Harold C., **14:**1212, *1213,* **14E:**500; **15:551,** *551*

U.S.S.R., *see* Soviet Union

Utah, **6:**527–29

Utah Beach, **15:**1282–83

Utrecht, Treaty of (1713), **2:**128, 130, **2E:**59, **69–70**

U-2 incident, **16:**1417

V

Vaca de Castro, Cristobal, **1E:35**

Valentine's Day massacre (1929), **13:***1154;* **14E:**489

Valentino, Rudolph, **13:***1148,* 1149, **13E:477,** *477*

Vallandigham, Clement, **8E:294–95**

Vallejo, Mariano, **6:**522

Valley Forge, **3E:108,** *108*

Van Buren, Martin, **5:**394, 396, *403,* **5E:183–84;** **6:**520; **7:**551
  Indians and, **5E:158**
  as vice president, **5:**402

Vance, Cyrus, **18:**1544

Vandenberg, Arthur Hendrick, **14E:515,** *515*

Vanderbilt, Cornelius, **10:**836, *862,* **10E:368–69,** *369*

Vanderbilt, William H., **10:***861–63*

Vanderbilt, William Henry, **10E:369**

Vanderbilt, William K., **11:**906

Van Devanter, Willis, **14:**1254, 1257, 1258, **14E:515–16**

Van Druten, John, **16:**1399

Vane, Sir Henry, **2E:71**

Van Rensselaer, Kiliaen, **1E:35**

Vanzetti, Bartolomeo, *see* Sacco-Vanzetti case

Vaquero, **9:***742–43*

Vassall, William, **2E:71**

Vassar, Matthew, **6E:204**

Vatican II Council, **17E:626**

Venezuela, **12:**996, 1026–27, **12E:**416, 430

Venezuela boundary dispute, **12E:441**

Venezuela Claims, **12E:441**

Veracruz, **7:***572–73*

Vermont, **3E:**77, 89

Verrazano, Giovanni da, **1:**19, *19,* **1E:35–36,** *35*

Versailles, Treaty of (1919), **13:1101–4,** **13E:475–76,** *476* (map)

Vesey, Denmark, **6E:220**

Vespucci, Amerigo, **1:**19, **1E:36,** *36*

Veterans
  G.I. Bill of Rights, **16E:568**
  Society of the Cincinnati, **3E:81**
  Vietnam, **18:**1536

Veterans Bureau scandal (1921), **13:**1123

Vice-President, **4:**288, 338

Viceroys, **1:**42–43

Vicksburg, **8:***649,* 649–51, 654, 671, *688, 691, 692*

Victoria, Queen of England, **11E:403**

Victorian furniture and furnishings, **11:***947–53, 956–57*

Viet Cong, **17:**1445

Vietnam, **16:**1390; **18:**1536–37
  refugees ("boat people"), **18:**1546
  see also Vietnam War

Vietnam veterans, **18:**1536

Vietnam War, **17:***1444,* **1445–71,** *1448, 1459–71,* **17E:**629; **18:**1535
  Agent Orange, **17E:1529**
  antiwar movement, **17:**1449–50, *1451,* 1475, **17E:**613
  fall of Saigon, **17E:604**
  Gulf of Tonkin Resolution, **17:**1446–47, **17E:608**
  invasion of Cambodia, **17E:609–10**
  invasion of Laos, **17E:610–11**
  My Lai massacre, **17:**1447, 1449
  Nixon's policy, **17:1474–75,** 1478–79
  peace agreement, **17:1482–83**
  Tet offensive, **17:**1451–53, *1468–69,* **17E:625–26**

Viking probes, **17:**1500

Vikings, **1E:36–37,** 20–21, 25–26

Villa, Pancho, **12:***1034,* **12E:441–42;** **13E:**471

Virginia, **3:**248, 250, **3E:**86
  American Revolution and, **3E:**93
  colonial, **1:71–73;** **2:**95, *146, 148–49*
  constitution of, **3:**246, 247, *247*

Virginia, University of (Charlottesville), **4:***294–95*

Virginia City, Montana, **9:**731, 735, *736,* 737, 740

Virginia Company of London, **1E:37**

Virginia dynasty, **4:**338

Virginia Plan, **4:***284,* 286, **4E:146**

Virginia Resolves, **2:**157–58, 164, **2E:71,**

VISTA (Volunteers in Service to America), **16:**1426

Voting age, **17E:626**

Voting rights, **4:**276
   of blacks, **8:**703–4, 706
   in revolutionary era, **3:**246–48
   of women, **4:**276
Voting Rights Act of 1965, **17E:**600

W

Wade, Benjamin F., **8:**645, 648, 701, *702*, **8E:295**
Wadsworth, James W., **15:**1268, **15E:551**
Wagner Act, *see* National Labor Relations Act
Wagner-Connery Act, **14:**1247
Wagon Box battle, **9:**782, 793, *793*
Wainwright, Jonathan Mayhew, **15E:**551–52, *552*
Wald, Lillian D., **12:**1055, **12E:442**
Waldseemüller, Martin, **1E:37**
Walke, Henry, **8E:295**
Walker, James, **7E:257**
Walker, William, **6E:220**
Wallace, George C., **17:**1454, 1458, **17E:**626–27
Wallace, Henry, **14:**1185
Wallace, Henry A., **13E:453**; **14:**1185, 1239–40, *1240*, **14E:516**, *516*; **16:**1364
Wallace, Henry C., **13:**1121, **13E:477**
Wallace, Lewis ("Lew"), **11E:403**
Wall Street volatility, **18E:**665–66
Walsh, Francis Patrick ("Frank"), **13:**1096, **13E:**477–78
Walsh, Thomas J., **13:**1124, 1126, **13E:478**
Walters, Henry, **11E:**403–4
Wampanoag Indians, **2E:**57–58, 73
Ward, Artemas, **3E:108**
Ward, Montgomery, **10:**853
War Finance Corporation, **13:**1130
War hawks, **4:**344–45
Warhol, Andy, **16:***1380–83*
War Industries Bond, **13E:449**
War Labor Disputes Act, **15:**1336
War Manpower Commission, **15:**1337
Warneford, Lieutenant Reginald, **13:***1113*
Warner, Charles Dudley, **11:**905, **11E:404**
War of 1812, **4:317**, *318–31*, **344–49**, *345, 346, 349*, **4E:**138
   results of, **5:**365
War of the Austrian Succession (King George's War), **2:**131
War of the Spanish Succession (Queen Anne's War), **2:**127
War Production Board, **15:**1336
Warren, Earl, **16:***1421*, **16E:592**, *592*; **17E:627**
Warren, Joseph, **3E:**108–9
Warren Commission, **17E:**627–28
Warsaw Uprising, **16E:570**
Washington, Booker T., **11:***961*, 963–64
Washington, Booker Taliaferro, **11E:404**

Washington, D.C., **4E:146,** 131
Washington, George, **2:**132; **3:**196, *242–43*, 262, 264, **3E:109**, *109*; **4:**275, *278–79*, 282, **4E:146–47**, *147*; **11:***923*; **18:***1593*, 1597, *258–59*
   American Revolution and, **3:**186–87, 189
   American Revolution and, **3:**211–13, *214-15*, 217, 219, 220, 223
   cherry tree legend, **5E:**184–85
   Constitution and, **4:**285, 290
   Peale's portrait of, **4:**351, *357*
   as president, **4:**288, 290, 301–13, *302–3, 306–7*
      economy, **4:**304–8
      Farewell Address, **4E:147**
      Federalists and, **4:**309
      French Revolution and, **4:**309–12
      retirement, **4:**313
      trade and, **4:**312–13
Washington, Harold, **18:***1586*
Washington, Treaty of, **9E:**299, **331**
Washington Conference for the Limitation of Armament (1921–1922), **13:**1123, 1133–34
Washingtonians, **6E:**220–21, *221*
Washington, D.C., **4:**333, *334*
Watergate scandal, **17:1480–81**, *1483–84, 1519–28*, **17E:**628–29
Waters, Walter W., **14E:486**
Waterways, **5:**407, *407–21*
   canals, **5:***420–21*
Watkins, Francis C., **14:***1230*
Watson, James D., **17:**1512–13, *1513*
Watson, Thomas J., Jr., **15E:**552–53; **17:**1505–6
Wayne, Anthony, **3E:**109–10; **4:***310, 311*
Weapons
   nuclear, **15E:**551; **18:**1545
      testing of, **16E:**579–80
      see also Atomic bomb
   Revolutionary War, **3:***228–37*
   Whitney's manufacture of, **5:**446–47, *446, 447*
   see also Arms control and disarmament
Weaver, James B., **10:**856, **10E:369**
Webster, Daniel, **4:**285; **5:**393, 398, 445; **7:**553, *620*, **621–28**, *625, 627*, **7E:257**
Webster, Noah, **4E:147**
Webster-Ashburton Treaty, **6E:221**; **7:**625–26
Webster-Hayne Debate, **5E:184**
Weed, Thurlow, **7:**611, **7E:**257–58
Weeks, John Wingate, **13E:**478–79
Weems, Mason Locke, **5E:**184–85, *184*
Weinberger, Caspar Willard, **18E:**666–67
Weld, Theodore Dwight, **6:**492–93, **6E:221**
Welles, Gideon, **7E:258**
Welles, Orson, **14:**1226
Welles, Sumner, **15:**1274, **15E:553**, *553*
Wells, H. G., **14:**1226
Wells Fargo, **9E:332**, *332*
Wesbury vs. Sanders, **14E:485**

West, Benjamin, **3E:110,** *110;* **4:**351, 352, 356
West, the
  agriculture and, **5:**435
  character of, **5:**391, 393–94, 405
  Civil War and, **9:**725, 726
  expansion and settlement of, **2:**97, 98, 123–26;
      3:*249,* **3E:**110; **4:**285, 336–37, **4E:**138–39;
      5:368, 429–30; **10:845–50**
    barbed wire and, **9:**770, *771, 772*
    canals and, **5:**432–35, *432–34*
    conquest, **9:726–28**
    immigrants in, **9:**775–76; **10:**849–50, *851*
    Indians and, **9:726–27,** *727, 729*
    land legislation and, **10:**845–47
    lawlessness, **9:**728, *728,* 733
    migration, **6:455–68,** 515, 517–18, **524–29;**
      9:775–76
    pioneering spirit, **9:728–30**
    railroads, **5:**435–41, *436–39, 441*
    taming of the West, **9:***790,* **791–801**
    technology and, **10:**847–49, *848*
    waterways and, **5:**407, *408–21,* 434–35
  exploration of, **6:511–14**
  Indians and, **5:**397–98, **5E:158**
  Jackson and, **5:**396–98
  sectionalism and, **5:**374–75
  Spain and, **2:**124
  territories, **6:**465–67
  transportation and
    highways, **5:**428–32, *430, 431*
  War of 1812 and, **4:**344–45, 348
  see also Cattlemen; Cowboys; Homesteaders;
    specific territories and states
West Berlin, **16:**1418
West Indies, **1:**20, 44, 45
Westinghouse, George, **10:**821, 849, **10E:369–70**
Westinghouse electric company, **10E:**370
Westmoreland, William, **17E:629,** *629*
Weston, Thomas, **1:**76; **2:**95, **2E:71–72**
West Point, **3E:**77, **78,** 94
Weyler, Gen. Valeriano "Butcher," **12:**1005
Weyler, Valeriano, **12E:442**
Weymouth, Capt. George, **1:**72
Whaling, **7:***589–99*
Wharton, Edith Newbold Jones, **11E:404–5**
Wheatley, Phyllis, **3E:110,** *110*
Wheeler, Burton K., **13:**1124; **14:**1256; **15:**1270
Wheeler, Burton Kendall, **13E:479**
Wheeler, Joseph, **8E:295–96,** *295*
Whig Party, **5:**401, **7:**588
Whipper, William, **7E:258**
Whipple, Abraham, **2:***164,* **2E:72**
Whiskey Rebellion, **4:**306, **4E:147–48**
Whiskey Ring, **8E:296**
Whistler, James Abbott McNeil, **11E:405–6,** *405*
White, Edward H., II, **17:***1493,* **17E:**597
White, John, **1E:**32; **2E:72**

White, Rev. John, **2:**95
White, John, **9:**734
White, William Allen, **10:860**
White Antelope, **9:***780,* 781
White-collar class, **12:**1050
Whitehead, Mary Beth, **18E:**634–35
Whiteman, Paul, **14E:495**
White William Allen, **14E:516–17,** *517*
Whitman, Walt, **11:***966,* 970, **11E:406,** *406*
Whitney, Eli, **5:***379,* 442, **443–48,** *444–47,* **5E:185;**
  10:818
  cotton gin, **5:***378, 442,* **443–46,** *445;* **7:**582–83
Whitridge, Arnold, **5:**443–48
Whittier, John Greenleaf, **6:**491, **6E:221–22**
Wigglesworth, Michael, **2E:72**
Wilhelm II, **13:479–80,** *479*
Wilkes, Charles, **6E:222**
Wilkinson, James, **3E:110–11**
Willard, Frances, **11:**946
Willard, Frances Elizabeth, **11E:406–7**
William I, Emperor of Germany, **9E:**331
William of Orange, **2:**126
Williams, Roger, **2:**97–98, *98,* 176, 177, **2E:72–73,** *73*
Williams, Tennessee, **16:**1399
Williamsburg, Va., **2:***137*
Willkie, Wendell L., **15:**1268
Willkie, Wendell Lewis, **15E:553–54,** *554*
Wilmot, David, **7:**550, **7E:258**
Wilmot Proviso, **7:**550, **7E:258–59**
Wilson, (Thomas) Woodrow, **12E:442–43,** *442;*
  13E:480
Wilson, Alexander, **4E:148**
Wilson, James, **3:***248,* **3E:111; 18:**1591
Wilson, Woodrow, **10:**855, 897–98, *898;*
  12:1035–36, 1053
Wilson-Gorman Tariff, **10E:370**
Wilson Tariff of 1894, **10:**880
Wimar, Charles, **6E:222**
Winder, William Henry, **4E:148**
Windmills, **9:**770
Windsor, Duke of, **14:**1225
Winslow, Edward, **1:***61;* **2:**173, **2E:73**
Winslow, John Ancrum, **8E:296**
Winslow, Josiah, **2:***176*
Winthrop, John, **1E:**29; **2:**96, *97, 170,* 173, 174, 176,
  2E:71, **73–74**
Winthrop, John (son), **2E:**48
Wirt, William, **5E:185**
Wisconsin, **6:**459
Wister, Owen, **11:**971–72, **11E:407**
Witherspoon, James, **3E:111,** *111*
Wolcott, Oliver, **5:**446
Wolfe, James, **2E:74**
Wolfe, Maj. Gen. James, **2:**118, 119, *120–21*
Wolfson, Louis E., **17E:606**
Women
  in 19th century, **6:**491, **6E:**193, 216; **9E:**303–4

Women, in 19th century (*cont.*)
    Civil War, **8E:**266, 269, 275, 280
      Molly Maguires, **9E:319**
      outlaws, **9E:**301–2, 330
    in American Revolution, **3E:**98–99
    in aviation, **14E:**492; **16E:**587
    black, **16E:**560
      in literature, **3E:**110
    education of, **11:**942
    in English colonies, **1:**64, 66
    Equal Rights Amendment (ERA), **18:**1538–39,
      18E:643
    industrialization and, **5:**427–28, *429*
    in labor force, **12:1064–66**
    literature and, **5E:172–73**
    Mann Act and, **12:**1055–56, **12E:**428–29
    National Organization for Women (NOW),
      17E:622–23
    property inheritance and, **3:**250
    Red Cross and, **9E:**300
    in reform movements, **11:946**
    right to life/pro-choice debate, **18E:662**
    in Senate, **14E:**489
    in space, **17:***1487*
    suffrage (voting rights), **4:**276; **9E:**300; **11:**946,
      11E:391–92; **12:**1064
    see also individual women
Women's Christian Temperance Movement,
    11:946, **11E:407**
Wood, Col. Leonard, **12:**1008
Wood, Fernando, **8E:296**
Wood, Grant, **14:**1227, **14E:517**
Wood, Leonard, **12E:443**
Woodford, Stewart Lyndon, **12E:443–44**
Woodrow Wilson, **13:***1084*, 1128, **13E:**452
    World War I and, **13:**1085–91, **1099–1104,** *1103,*
      13E:475–76
Woodruff, Theodore Tuttle, **10:**820, **10E:370**
Woodson, Samuel, **6:**525
Woodstock, **17E:629**
Woodward, Bob, **17:**1480
Wool, John Ellis, **7E:259**
Worcester, Samuel Austin, **5E:185**
Worcester vs. Georgia, **5:**397, **5E:185**
Workers
    in 19th century, **6:**487–88
    in 1920s, **13:**1131–33
    in 1930s, **14:**1247
    migrant laborers, **16:**1416, 1426; **17E:**599;
      18E:650
    Triangle fire, **12E:440–41**
    women, **12:1064–66**
    World War I and, **13:**1096–97
    World War II and, **15:**1336, 1337
    see also Labor; Labor Unions
Works Progress Administration (WPA), **14:**1243,
    1248
World Court, **13:**1133; **14:**1211, 1221

World Disarmament Conference (1932),
    14:1215–16
World Economics Conference (1933), **13E:**454
World War I, **10:**889, 898; **12:**1053; **13:1085–1117,**
    13E:447–48, 454–55, 471,
    air warfare, **13:***1105–17*
    home front, **13:1094–101**
    peace talks, **13:**1100–1
    U.S. role in, **13:**1090–92
    Versailles Treaty (1919), **13:1101–4, 13E:475–76,**
      476 (map)
    Zimmermann note and, **13E:**481
World War II
    in Africa, **15:**1296–97, **15:***1303* (map)
    China and, **15:**1274
    D-Day, **15:***1275–89, 1280–81* (map)
    demobilization after, **16:**1357–58
    economy of the U.S. after, **16:**1355–56
    Eisenhower in, **15:**1276, 1296, **15E:529–30**
    France in, **15:**1266, 1268, 1302
    Germany in, **15:**1268, 1270–73, 1291–92, **1301–5,**
      1296–97, **15E:**532–33
    Great Britain in, **15:**1266, 1268–72, 1301, 1302,
      1304
    home front, **15:1335–38**
    Italy in, **15:**1291, 1296–98, 1301
    Japan in, **15:**1274, **1291–96, 1298–1301,** *1298,*
      1299, **1305–10,** 1333, **15E:**537–38
    Lendlease program, **15:**1269–70
    maps
      Africa and Europe, **15:***1303*
      D-Day, **15:***1280–81*
      the Pacific, **15:***1299*
    neutrality of U.S. (1939–41), **15:**1266–67
    Nuremberg trials after, **15E:**534–35, *535*
    in the Pacific, **15:1291–96, 1298–1301,** *1298,*
      1299, **1305–10, 15E:**536–37,
    the Philippines in, **15:**1291–92, 1298, 1306–9,
      15E:536–37
    preparedness of U.S., **15:**1268
    Franklin D. Roosevelt and, **15:1266–74,** 1291,
      1296, *1332,* 1333, 1334, 1338
    the Soviet Union in, **15:**1266, 1270, 1271,
      1292–93, 1304
    submarines in, **15:**1273
    U.S. Navy in, **15:**1291–92
    workers and, **15:**1336, 1337
    see also individual leaders and generals, specific
      countries, and battles
Wounded Knee (South Dakota), seizure of (1973),
    17E:596
Wounded Knee Massacre, **9:**799, **9E:333,** *333*
Wovoka (Jack Wilson), **9:**799, **9E:**312
Wozniak, Stephen, **17:***1507,* 1507
WPA (Works Progress Administration), **14:**1243,
    1428
Wright, Frank Lloyd, **11:**976; **14E:517–18,** *518*
Wright, Jim, **18:**1569

Wright Brothers, **12**:1060, *1062–63*, **12E:444,** *444*
Writs of Assistance, **2E:**62
Wynkoop, Maj. E. W., **9:**781

X

XYZ Affair, **4:**314, *315*, **4E:148,** *148*

Y

Yale University, **14:**1212
Yalta Conference (1945), **15:***1332,* 1333–34,
    15E:554–55, *555*
Yamamoto, Fleet Admiral Isoroku, **15:**1294,
    15E:555, *555*
Yancey, William Lowndes, **7E:**259
Yeager, Chuck, **16E:**587
Yellow fever, **12E:**432
Yellow journalism, **11E:**395–96

York, Alvin, **13E:480**
Yorktown, Battle of, **3:**222, *222–23,* 226, **3E:**83, 85,
    106
Young, Andrew, **18:**1544, 1547, 1552
Young, Brigham, **6:**528, *528,* **6E:222**
Young, John W., **17:**1492, **17E:**597
Younger, (Thomas) Coleman, **10E:370**
Younger, Bob, **10:***839*
Younger, Cole, **10:**839
Yugoslavia, **13:**1102

Z

Zangara, Giuseppe, **14E:**491
Zapata, Emiliano, **12:***1034*, **12E:444**
Zenger, John Peter, **2E:74,** *74*
Ziegfeld, Florenz, **13E:480–81,** *481*
Zimmermann, Arthur, **13:**1090, **13E:**481
Zimmerman note, **13E:481**
Zuñi pueblos, **1E:**10

BIBLIOGRAPHY

Compiled by Betty H. Grebey

GRADE LEVELS:
M = Middle School (Grades 5–8)
J = Junior High School (Grades 7–9)
H = High School (Grades 9–12)
A = Adult
F indicates a work of fiction, poetry, or drama.

A

America's Outdoor Wonders: State Parks and Sanctuaries. Washington: National Geographic, 1987. (J,H,A) Describes a sampling of the wilderness areas.

Archer, Jules. *The Incredible Sixties: The Stormy Years That Changed America*. New York: Harcourt Brace, 1986. (M,J,H) Analyzes the 1960s and the significant events and individuals that transformed U.S. society.

Arnold, Caroline. *The Golden Gate Bridge*. New York: Watts, 1986. (M,J) Details the story of the engineering, construction, and changes of the famous bridge.

Ashby, LeRoy. *William Jennings Bryan: Champion of Democracy*. Schenectady, NY: Twayne, 1987. (H,A) Describes Bryan's life and shows how he kept traditional social values alive while striving for a greater democracy for the common people.

B

Ballard, Robert D. *Exploring the Titanic*. New York: Scholastic, 1988. (M,J,H) Accurately details the *Titanic*'s fatal voyage and the exploration of the wreck 74 years later.

Bigler, Philip. *Washington in Focus: The Photo History of the Nation's Capital*. Arlington, VA: Vandimere, 1988. (H,A) Covers the period from the site placement compromise of 1792 to the present.

Birnbaum, Louis. *Red Dawn at Lexington*. Boston: Houghton Mifflin, 1986. (H,A) An account of the opening battles of the American Revolution.

Black, Sheila. *Sitting Bull*. Englewood Cliffs, NJ: Silver Burdett, 1989. (J,H) Recounts the chief's heroic struggle for freedom, victory at Little Big Horn, and death in the 1890 Sioux uprising.

Blockson, Charles. *The Underground Railroad: First-Person Narratives of Escape to Freedom in the North*. Englewood Cliffs, NJ: Prentice Hall, 1987. (H,A) Introduces runaway slaves and conductors and agents of the underground railroad through their narratives.

Blumberg, Rhoda. *The Incredible Journey of Lewis and Clark*. New York: Lothrop, Lee & Shepard, 1987. (M,J) Describes how Lewis and Clark explored western regions of America in the early 19th century.

Blumenson, Martin. *Patton, the Man Behind the Legend: 1885–1945*. New York: Morrow, 1985. (H,A) Studies the character and life of one of the world's greatest generals.

Bober, Natalie E. *Thomas Jefferson: Man on a Mountain*. New York: Atheneum, 1988. (M,J,H) Comprehensive, well-documented, and very readable biography with chronology.

Boffey, Philip M., ed. *Claiming the Heavens: The New York Times Complete Guide to the Star Wars Debate*. New York: Times Books, 1988. (H,A) Presents political, technological, and military issues of the SDI.

Bolger, Daniel P. *Americans at War, 1975–1986: An Era of Violent Peace*. Novato, CA: Presidio, 1988. (H,A) Studies eight uses of U.S. military force in the post-Vietnam era.

Boorstin, Daniel J. *The Landmark History of the American People*. Rev. ed. New York: Random House, 1987. (M,J,H) Chronicles the spirit, ingenuity, and accomplishments of Americans, from the pioneers to the present.

Branch, Taylor. *Parting the Waters: America in the King Years, 1954–1963*. New York: Simon & Schuster, 1988. (H,A) An overview of the civil rights movement, focusing on Martin Luther King, Jr. and other individuals in the movement.

Bruchey, Stuart. *The Wealth of the Nation: An Economic History of the United States*. New York: Harper & Row, 1987. (H,A) Analyzes American economic history, from Colonial times through the 1929 crash to Kennedy's tax cuts.

Burchard, Sue. *The Statue of Liberty: Birth to Rebirth*. New York: Harcourt Brace, 1985. (M,J,H) Traces the history of the statue and describes the restoration project and the statue's changing symbolism.

Burner, David. *John F. Kennedy and a New Generation*. Boston: Little, Brown, 1988. (H,A) An impartial overview of Kennedy and his presidency.

Burns, James MacGregor. *The Workshop of Democracy*. New York: Knopf, 1985. (H,A) Traces the history of the United States from the Emancipation Proclamation through the Depression.

C

Cannon, Devereaux D. *The Flags of the Confederacy: An Illustrated History*. Wrightville Beach, NC: St. Luke's/Broadfoot, 1988. (H,A) Charts the evolution of the many battle flags, the "Stars and Bars," the Confederate flag of 1865, and the individual state flags.

Civil War. Alexandria, VA: Time-Life, 1983–1987. 28 vols. (J,H,A) A pictorial history that covers the conflict from its causes to the final surrender.

Clapp, Patricia. *The Tamarack Tree: A Novel of the Siege of Vicksburg*. New York: Lothrop, Lee & Shepard, 1986. (M,J) A teenage English girl becomes trapped in the 47-day siege of Vicksburg in 1863. F

Claypool, Jane. *The Worker in America*. New York: Watts, 1985. (J,H) Examines the history of American labor—the colonial agrarian society, the union movements, and the hightech industry of today.

Clifton, James A. *The Potawatomi*. New York, Chelsea House, 1987. (M,J) Examines the history of this Plains Indian tribe and their present life and struggle to keep their heritage.

Coffey, Vincent J. *The Battle of Gettysburg*. Englewood Cliffs, NJ: Silver Burdett, 1986. (J,M,H) Recounts the events, strategies, and personalities of the 1863 Civil War battle that devastated Union troops and left both sides in despair.

Cooke, Alistair. *America Observed: From the 1940's to the 1980's*. New York: Knopf, 1988. (H,A) These 58 articles provide an overview of the cultural, political, and social mores of the American people.

Cooper, Ilene. *Susan B. Anthony*. New York: Watts, 1984. (M,J) Details her life, impact on 19th-century America, and advocacy of women's suffrage.

Corbin, Carole Lynn. *The Right to Vote*. New York: Watts, 1985. (J,H) Chronicles the 200-year struggle of women and minority groups to gain the right to vote.

Corcoran, Barbara. *The Sky Is Falling*. New York: Atheneum, 1988. (J,H) Set in Boston in 1931; a young girl adjusts to a new life after her father loses his job in the Depression. F

Costabel, Eva Deutsch. *The Pennsylvania Dutch: Craftsmen and Farmers*. New York: Macmillan, 1986. (M,J) Introduces the lifestyle and crafts of the Pennsylvania Dutch.

Cwiklik, Robert. *King Philip*. Englewood Cliffs, NJ: Silver Burdett, 1989. (J,H) Chronicles the life of the chief of the Wampanoags and the tribe's war on the New England colonies.

Cwiklik, Robert. *Sequoyah*. Englewood Cliffs, NJ: Silver Burdett, 1989. (J,H) Details the life of the leader of the Cherokee tribe, focusing on his creation of the Cherokee language and alphabet.

D

Davis, Burke. *The Long Surrender*. New York: Random House, 1985. (H,A) Details the collapse of the Confederacy and the flight of Jefferson Davis and his cabinet as they try to escape capture.

Davis, Sam. *A Miner's Christmas Card and Other Frontier Tales*. Santa Cruz, CA: Western Tanager, 1987. (H,A) Colorful tales of frontier life and the mining camps.

De Ford, Deborah H. *An Enemy Among Them*. Boston: Houghton Mifflin, 1987. (J) In this romance set during the Revolutionary War, Margaret falls in love with the Hessian soldier who wounded her brother. F

Devaney, John. *Franklin Delano Roosevelt, President*. New York: Watts, 1987. (M,J) Traces Roosevelt's four-term presidency through the Depression and World War II.

Diggins, John Patrick. *The Proud Decades: America in War and Peace, 1941–1960*. New York: Norton, 1988. (H,A) Covers the 1940s through the 1950s—from foreign policy to popular culture.

Dillon, Eilis. *The Seekers*. New York: Scribner's, 1986. (J) Based on firsthand accounts, this novel portrays the tribulations of a teenage couple who leave England and settle in the New World in 1632. F

Dolan, Edward F. *Victory in Europe: The Fall of Hitler's Germany*. New York: Watts, 1988. (J,H) Presents a detailed account of the last seven months of World War II in Europe, including major battles, the death camps, and important agreements.

Dorris, Michael. *A Yellow Raft in Blue Water*. New York: Holt, 1987. (H,A) Follows three generations of Indian women and their struggles. F

Dugan, Clark, et al. *The American Experience in Vietnam*. New York: Norton, 1988. (H,A) Provides eyewitness and historical accounts of the U.S. involvement in Vietnam, including the problems on the home front.

E

Edelman, Bernard, ed. *Dear America: Letters Home from Vietnam*. New York: Norton, 1985. (H,A) Letters reveal the frustration, pain, and anger of soldiers and civilians in Vietnam.

Ehle, John. *Trail of Tears: The Rise and Fall of the Cherokee Nation*. New York: Anchor, 1988. (H,A) Recounts the history of the Cherokee nation, the development of their society, and the factors leading to the 1838 migration.

Elliott, Emery, ed. *Columbia Literary History of the United States*. New York: Columbia University Press, 1988. (H,A) Presents literary genres, assesses trends, and gives critical perspectives for American literature.

Eyes on the Prize Production Team, The. *Eyes on the Prize: America's Civil Rights Years*. New York: Penguin, 1987. (H,A) This illustrated documentary history examines the background of the civil rights movement with firsthand accounts of participants.

F

Faber, Doris, and Harold Faber. *We the People: The Story of the U.S. Constitution Since 1787*. New York: Scribner's, 1987. (J,H) Looks at the story behind the making and ratifying of the Constitution and its impact through the years.

Feldbaum, Carl B., and Ronald J. Bree. *Looking the Tiger in the Eye: Confronting the Nuclear Threat*. New York: Harper & Row, 1988. (H,A) Gives the history of nuclear weapons, including decisions made by political, military, and scientific officials.

Ferraro, Geraldine A. *Ferraro: My Story*. New York: Bantam, 1985. (H,A) Discusses how the first woman to be nominated by a major party for the vice-presidency of the U.S. made her way.

Ferrell, Robert H. *Woodrow Wilson and World War I, 1917–1921*. New York: Harper & Row, 1985. (H,A) Examines Wilson as president and his inability to secure passage of the Treaty of Versailles.

Fisher, Dorothy Canfield. *Our Independence and the Constitution*. New York: Random House, 1987. (M,J) Depicts the writing of the Declaration of Independence and the Constitution as seen by a Philadelphia family.

Fisher, Leonard Everett. *The Alamo*. New York: Holiday House, 1987. (M,J) Details the history of the Alamo from its days as a mission to its famous battle.

Fisher, Leonard Everett. *Ellis Island: Gateway to the New World*. New York: Holiday House, 1986. (M,J) Describes the site where the immigrants from Europe entered the U.S. from 1892 to 1954.

Flanagan, Mike. *Out West*. New York: Abrams, 1987. (H,A) Relates the stories behind the buffalo nickel, the Teapot Dome Scandal, the Gunfight at the O.K. Corral, and more.

Fox, Mary Virginia. *Mister President: The Story of Ronald Reagan*. Rev ed. Hillside, NJ: Enslow, 1986. (M,J) Describes various milestones in Reagan's life.

Freedman, Russell. *Cowboys of the Wild West*. Merlin, OR: Clarion, 1985. (M,J) Relates the

story of the American cowboys as they really were—young men who herded cattle and worked on the ranches.

Freedman, Russell. *Indian Chiefs*. New York: Holiday House, 1985. (M,J) The lives of six chiefs illustrate the dilemma faced by the Indians: fight or cooperate.

Freedman, Russell. *Lincoln: A Photobiography*. New York: Clarion, 1987. (M,J) A study of Lincoln's life through photographs, prints, and a sampling of his writings.

Fritz, Jean. *Make Way for Sam Houston*. New York: Putnam, 1986. (M,J) Chronicles the life of a man who was a lawyer, a general, president of the Republic of Texas, a senator, and governor of Texas.

G

Garrison, Webb. *A Treasury of Civil War Tales*. Nashville: Rutledge Hill, 1988. (H,A) A compendium of 57 Civil War tales.

Garrow, David J. *Bearing the Cross: Martin Luther King, Jr. and the Southern Christian Leadership Conference*. New York: Morrow, 1986. (H,A) A biography of King and an examination of the movement he led.

Giardina, Denise. *Storming Heaven*. New York: Norton, 1987. (H,A) A riveting story of radical politics and corporate greed based on the 1921 mine workers' rebellion in West Virginia. F

Glassman, Bruce. *The Crash of '29 and the New Deal*. New York: Silver Burdett, 1986. (M,J) Examines the period from the twenties to the financial reconstruction of the New Deal and World War II.

Goldstein, Toby. *Waking from the Dream: America in the Sixties*. Englewood Cliffs, NJ: Julian Messner, 1988. (M,H) A provocative look at U.S. social programs in the 1960s: where they succeeded and failed.

Good, Merle. *Who Are the Amish?* Intercourse, PA: Good Books, 1985. (H,A) Describes the history, life, and culture of the Amish and how they interact with the world.

Gordon, Lois. *American Chronicles: Six Decades in American Life, 1920-1980*. New York: Atheneum, 1987. (H,A) Provides yearly coverage on news, ads, music, movies, theater, art, books, science, fashion, sports, and technology.

Gorman, Carol. *America's Farm Crisis*. New York: Watts, 1987. (M,J) Presents the history of U.S. farming since the 1960s and describes the effect of the crisis on our population.

Granzotto, Gianni. *Christopher Columbus*. Norman, OK: University of Oklahoma Press, 1988. (H,A) Traces the life of the explorer and the abilities that brought him to the New World.

H

Hamilton, Virginia. *The People Could Fly: American Black Folktales*. New York: Knopf, 1985. (M,J) Collected black American folktales about animals, fantasy, and the desire for freedom. F

Hanmer, Trudy J. *The Advancing Frontier*. New York: Watts, 1986. (M,J) Traces the history of westward expansion in U.S.

Hanmer, Trudy J. *The Growth of Cities*. New York: Watts, 1985. (M,J) Chronicles the growth and problems of American cities.

Hansbury, Lorraine. *A Raisin in the Sun*. New York: NAL, 1961. (J,H,A) This drama of a black family in 1950s Chicago shows the economic and social plight of blacks on the eve of the civil rights movement. F

Hargrove, Jim. *Daniel Boone, Pioneer Trailblazer*. Chicago: Children's, 1985. (J) Traces the life of the colonial pioneer and woodsman from his childhood to his wilderness adventures.

Harlan, Judith. *American Indians Today: Issues and Conflicts*. New York: Watts, 1987. (J,H) Analyzes the issues now facing Native Americans, including the conflict between traditional Indian and non-Indian beliefs.

Harr, John Ensor, and Peter J. Johnson. *The Rockefeller Century*. New York: Scribner's, 1988. (H,A) Traces the Rockefeller legacy of philanthropy through three generations.

Harris, Jonathan. *A Statue for America: The First 100 Years of the Statue of Liberty*. New York: Four Winds, 1985. (J) Gives the history of the statue from its design to its erection.

Harrison, Daphne Duval. *Black Pearls: Blues Queens of the 1920's*. New Brunswick, NJ: Rutgers University Press, 1988. (H,A) Focuses on four influential blues singers: Sippie Wallace, Edith Wilson, Victoria Spivey, and Alberta Hunter.

Haskins, James. *Black Music in America: A History Through Its People*. New York: Crowell, 1987. (J,H) Examines the history of black music from the slave songs and spirituals to the music of today.

Haskins, James. *The 60s Reader*. New York: Viking Kestrel, 1988. (J,H) Essays, speeches, and reports that cover the upheavals of the 1960s.

Hauptly, Denis J. *"A Convention of Delegates": The Creation of the Constitution*. New York: Atheneum, 1987. (M,J) Decsribes the events of the convention at which the delegates struggled to form the U.S. Constitution.

Hawke, David Freeman. *Everyday Life in Early America*. New York: Harper & Row, 1988. (H,A) Presents the life of 17th-century Americans by describing farms, houses, health care, manners, and warfare.

Hawke, David Freeman. *Nuts and Bolts of the Past: A History of American Technology, 1776–1860*. New York: Harper & Row, 1988. (H,A) Depicts the nation's first 85 years of invention and industry.

Highwater, Jamake. *The Ceremony of Innocence*. New York: Harper & Row, 1985. (J,H) A Native American bears the child of a white trader and watches her grow up an outcast in both societies. F

Highwater, Jamake. *I Hear the Morning Star*. New York: Harper & Row, 1986. (J,H) A Native American learns to express his heritage through painting. F

Hokanson, Drake. *The Lincoln Highway: Main Street Across America*. Iowa City, IA: University of Iowa Press, 1988. (H,A) Presents an illustrated history of the first transcontinental automotive highway and the start of the U.S. auto craze.

The Homefront: America During World War II. Compiled by Mark Jonathan Harris, Franklin D. Mitchell, and Steven J. Schnecter. New York: Putnam, 1984. (H,A) Tells how World War II changed the United States and its people.

Hoyt, Edwin P. *The GI's War: The Story of American Soldiers in Europe in World War II*. New York: McGraw-Hill, 1988. (H,A) Focuses on the careers of a dozen soldiers who participated in heavy fighting in North Africa.

Hurt, Harry. *For All Mankind*. New York: Atlantic Monthly, 1988. (H,A) Recounts the history of the U.S. space program up to the Apollo moon landings.

Hurt, Henry. *Reasonable Doubt: An Investigation into the Assassination of John F. Kennedy*. New York: Holt, 1986. Assesses both the original and subsequent controversy surrounding Kennedy's assassination.

I

Irwin, Hadley. *Kim/Kimi*. New York: Margaret K. McElderry, 1987. (J,H) The reader learns about the internment of the Japanese-Americans during World War II as a young girl tries to find answers about her Japanese-American father. F

J

Jones, Douglas C. *Roman*. New York: Holt, 1986. (H) This novel about a boy leaving home in 1865 to make his way West is filled with true details about the westward movement. F

K

Kassem, Lou. *Listen for Rachel*. New York: Macmillan, 1986. (J) While Rachel is living with her grandparents in Appalachia, the beginning of the Civil War brings tragedy and romance into her life. F

Kaye, Tony. *Lyndon B. Johnson*. New York: Chelsea House, 1987. (M,J,H) Shows Johnson's capabilities as a senator, majority leader, and president.

Keller, Mollie. *Alexander Hamilton*. New York: Watts, 1986. (M,J) Illustrates the life of the man who helped draft the Constitution and served as the first Secretary of the Treasury.

Kherdian, David. *Bridger: The Story of a Mountain Man*. New York: Greenwillow, 1987. (M,J) Depicts Jim Bridger's expedition through more than 2,000 miles of wilderness and the discovery of the Great Salt Lake.

Kosof, Anna. *Homeless in America*. New York: Watts, 1988. (J,H) Examines the plight of America's homeless, causes, and government's responses.

Kozol, Jonathan. *Rachel and Her Children: Homeless Families in America*. New York: Crown, 1988. (H,A) Examines real situations from across the country to show the problem of the homeless.

Kurtzman, Joel. *The Decline and Crash of the American Economy*. New York: Norton, 1988. (H,A) Discusses the 1987 stock market crash, events leading to today's problems, and possible solutions.

L

Lacey, Robert. *Ford: The Man and the Machine*. Boston: Little, Brown, 1986, (H,A) Focuses on the lives of Henry Ford, his son Edsel, and his grandson Henry II.

Landau, Elaine. *Growing Old in America*. New York: Julian Messner, 1985. (J) Explores the problems, experiences, and special concerns of the elderly in America.

Landau, Elaine. *The Homeless*. New York: Julian Messner, 1987. (M,J) Discusses the conditions, causes, and possible solutions of America's homeless.

Larrabee, Eric. *Commander in Chief: Franklin Delano Roosevelt, His Lieutenants and Their War*. New York: Harper & Row, 1987. (A) Presents Roosevelt's military leadership, his choice of military leaders, and portraits of ten World War II commanders.

Lasky, Kathryn. *Beyond the Divide*. New York: Dell, 1987. (J) An Amish farmer and his daughter join a wagon train heading West and find themselves facing many troubles. F

Lavender, David. *The Way to the Western Sea: Lewis and Clark Across the Continent*. New York: Harper & Row, 1988. (H,A) Explains the politics and logistics of the Lewis and Clark expedition and portrays the people involved.

Lawler, Mary. *Marcus Garvey*. New York: Chelsea House, 1987. (J,A) Relates the life of the father of the black separatist movement from his birth in Jamaica to his founding of the Universal Negro Improvement Association.

Leavell, Perry J. *Harry S. Truman*. New York: Chelsea House, 1987. (M,J) Presents the life, times, and leadership of President Truman.

Lens, Sidney. *Strikemakers and Strikebreakers*. New York: Lodestar, 1985. (J) Surveys the history of U.S. labor unions and the purpose and effectiveness of strikes, and profiles labor leaders.

Lewis, Richard S. *Challenger: The Final Voyage*. New York: Columbia University Press, 1988. (H,A) A clear, balanced presentation of the space shuttle tragedy.

Limerick, Patricia Nelson. *The Legacy of Conquest: The Unbroken Past of the American West*. New York: Norton, 1987. (A) Presents the West as an area with a conflict between cultures, religions, languages, and property rights.

Lipman, Jean, et al. *Young America: A Folk-Art History*. New York: Hudson Hills/Museum of Folk Art, 1986. (H,A) Collected artwork and photographs depict how America lived, worked, and played from the Revolutionary War days to World War I.

Litwack, Leon A., and August Meier, eds. *Black Leaders of the Nineteenth Century*. Urbana, IL: University of Illinois Press, 1988. (H,A) Gives biographical essays of leaders in the struggle for racial equality.

Lord, Walter. *The Night Lives On*. New York: Morrow, 1986. (H,A) Presents new evidence and theories on the sinking of the *Titanic*.

M

McAuliffe, Christa. *"I Touch the Future . . . ": The Story of Christa McAuliffe*. New York: Random House, 1986. (H,A) Relates McAuliffe's life through her fame as the first teacher in the space program, and her tragic death in the Challenger disaster.

McCall, Edith. *Mississippi Steamboatman: The Story of Henry Miller Shreve*. New York: Walker, 1986. (J) Surveys the achievements of the inventor who built the first steamboat to sail upstream on the river.

McClard, Megan, and George Ypsilantis. *Hiawatha*. Englewood Cliffs, NJ: Silver Burdett, 1989. (J,M,H) Details the life of the chief of the Onandaga Indians.

McClung, Robert M. *The True Adventures of Grizzly Adams: A Biography*. New York: Morrow, 1985. (J,H) Details the life of Grizzly Adams as a hunter in the old West.

McCullough, David Willis, ed. *American Childhoods: An Anthology*. Boston: Little, Brown, 1987. (H,A) Excerpts from literary autobiography, from Benjamin Franklin to Maya Angelou.

McDonough, James Lee, and James Pickett Jones. *War So Terrible: Sherman and Atlanta*. New York: Norton, 1987. (H,A) Narrates Sherman's campaign for Atlanta in 1864.

McElvaine, Robert S. *The Great Depression: America, 1929–1941*. New York: Times Books, 1985. (H,A) This history of the Depression shows how poverty was eased by innovative labor, social, and arts programs.

McGowen, Tom. *George Washington*. New York: Watts, 1986. (M,J) Focuses on Washington's private life, military experiences, and presidency.

McKissack, Patricia. *The Civil Rights Movement in America from 1865 to the Present*. Chi-

cago: Children's, 1987. (M,J) Describes the black civil rights struggle and profiles the leaders of the movement.

MacNeil, Robert, ed. *The Way We Were: 1963, the Year Kennedy Was Shot*. New York: Carrol & Graf, 1988. (H,A) Gives a broad picture—the politics, people, and popular culture of 1963.

McPherson, James M. *Battle Cry of Freedom: The Era of the Civil War*. New York: Oxford, 1988. (H,A) Follows American history from the end of the Mexican War in 1848 to the end of the Civil War in 1865.

McPhillips, Martin. *The Constitutional Convention*. Englewood Cliffs, NJ: Silver Burdett, 1986. (M,J) Describes how delegates from the original states gathered to create a constitution.

Mapp, Alf J. *Thomas Jefferson: A Strange Case of Mistaken Identity*. Lanham, MD: Madison, 1987. (A) Reassesses Jefferson's character, impact, and actions.

Marrin, Albert. *1812, the War Nobody Won*. New York: Atheneum, 1983. (M,J) Describes the reasons for the war, its major battles, and its settlement.

Marrin, Albert. *Struggle for a Continent: The French and Indian Wars, 1690–1760*. New York: Atheneum, 1987. (M,J) Discusses the history of the French and Indian Wars, the leaders, and the implications.

Marrin, Albert. *War Clouds in the West: Indians and Cavalrymen, 1860–1890*. New York: Atheneum, 1984. (J) Describes the battles between the U.S. Army and the Indians during the settlement of the West.

Marrin, Albert. *The Yanks Are Coming: The United States in the First World War*. New York: Atheneum, 1986. (J) Details the U.S. experience in World War I, from the homefront to the trench warfare in Europe.

Mee, Charles. *The Genius of the People*. New York: Harper & Row, 1987. (H,A) Recreates the writing of the U.S. Constitution through the debates, quarrels, and compromises that took place.

Meltzer, Milton, ed. *The American Revolutionaries: A History in Their Own Words, 1750–1800*. New York: Crowell, 1987. (M,J) A collection of eyewitness accounts, diary excerpts, and letters, giving an account of the rebel point of view.

Meltzer, Milton, ed. *The Black Americans: A History in Their Own Words*. New York: Crowell, 1984. (M,J) Records the history of the black experience in America from 1619 to the present.

Meltzer, Milton. *Poverty in America*. New York: Morrow, 1986. (J,H) Looks at the problems of hunger, homelessness, and unemployment.

Miller, Douglas T. *Frederick Douglass and the Flight for Freedom*. New York: Facts on File, 1988. (J,H) Integrates Douglass's personal story with the political events of his time, focusing on his struggle for freedom.

Miller, Marilyn. *The Bridge at Selma*. Englewood Cliffs, NJ: Silver Burdett, 1985. (M,J) Describes the repercussions of the events of March 7, 1965, when 525 people tried to march from Selma to the state capitol at Montgomery to register to vote.

Miller, Marilyn. *D-Day*. Englewood Cliffs, NJ: Silver Burdett, 1986. (M,J) Describes the Allied invasion of France from the Normandy beaches on June 6, 1944.

Miller, Marilyn. *The Transcontinental Railroad*. Englewood Cliffs, NJ: Silver Burdett, 1985. (M,J) Describes the construction of the Central Pacific, the Union Pacific, and related railroads.

Mills, Judie. *John F. Kennedy*. New York: Watts, 1988. (J,H) A thorough biography and evaluation of Kennedy's life and years in office.

Mitchell, Reid. *Civil War Soldiers*. New York: Viking, 1988. (H,A) Provides a cultural portrait of Northern and Southern soldiers.

Morris, Charles R. *Iron Destinies, Lost Opportunities: The Arms Race Between the USA and the USSR, 1945–1987*. New York: Harper & Row, 1988. (H,A) Covers the history of strategic confrontation between the superpowers.

Morris, Richard B. *The Forging of the Union, 1781–1789*. New York: Harper & Row, 1987. (H,A) Looks at the history of the United States between the end of the Revolution and the establishment of the federal government.

Morris, Richard B. *Witnesses at the Creation: Hamilton, Madison, Jay, and the Constitution*. New York: Holt, 1985. (H,A) Focuses on the creation and ramifications of the Constitution.

Morrison, Toni. *Beloved: A Novel*. New York: Knopf, 1987. (H,A) An escaped slave living in post-Civil War Ohio is haunted by memories. F

Murray, Robert A. *The Bozeman Trail: Highway of History*. Boulder, CO: Pruett, 1988. (H,A) Describes the events and locations along the historic trail, highlighting military and pioneer aspects.

Murrow, Liza Ketchum. *West Against the Wind.* New York: Holiday House, 1987. (M,J) A wilderness survival story of 14-year-old Abigail Parker's cross-country trip to California in 1850. F

O

Oakley, J. Ronald. *God's Country: America in the Fifties.* New York: Dembner, 1986. (H,A) Examines the history of the 1950s, the presidencies of Truman and Eisenhower, and influential people, events, and movements of the decade.

Ochoa, George. *The Fall of Mexico City.* Englewood Cliffs, NJ: Silver Burdett, 1989. (J, M,H) An account of the Texan Revolt, the Mexican War, and their social and political effects on U.S and Latin American history.

O'Dell, Scott. *The Serpent Never Sleeps: A Novel of Jamestown and Pocahontas.* New York: Houghton Mifflin, 1987. (M,J) Life in colonial Jamestown is shown through the story of Serena and her friendship with Pocahontas. F

O'Dell, Scott. *Streams to the River, River to the Sea.* Boston: Houghton Mifflin, 1986. (J) The story of the Indian girl who was interpreter for the Lewis and Clark expedition. F

Olson, James S. *Historical Dictionary of the 1920s: From World War I to the New Deal, 1919–1933.* Westport, CT: Greenwood, 1988. (H,A) Focuses on the events of the 1920s in the U.S. and includes more than 700 biographical entries, legal cases, and social issues.

Opie, John. *The Law of the Land: Two Hundred Years of American Farmland Policy.* Lincoln, NE: University of Nebraska Press, 1987. (H,A) Chronicles the 200-year history of U.S. public land policy to 20th-century land conservation trends and recent actions designed to protect agricultural land.

P

Packard, Vance. *The Ultra Rich: How Much Is Too Much?* Boston: Little, Brown, 1988. (H,A) Examines the very wealthy and the impact of wealth on the American economy.

Paine, Thomas, and Thomas Jefferson. *Paine and Jefferson on Liberty.* New York: Ungar, 1988. (H,A) Collects the most quoted works of these two men whose writings played an important part in the American Revolution.

Painter, Nell Irvin. *Standing at Armaggedon: The United States, 1877–1919.* New York: Norton, 1987. (H,A) Examines the years of growth, technological progress, and reform as America changed from an agrarian society to an industrial one.

Palmer, Dave Richard, and James W. Stryker. *Early American Wars and Military Institutions.* Garden City Park, NY: Avery, 1987. (H,A) Covers the battles, campaigns, organization, economy, and relationships with society of American armies from the Revolution to the beginning of the Civil War.

Patton, Phil. *Open Road: A Celebration of the American Highway.* New York: Simon & Schuster, 1986. (H,A) Gives the history, engineering, and mythology of the American highway.

Paters, William. *A More Perfect Union: The Men and Events That Made the Constitution.* New York: Crown, 1987. (H,A) Discusses the creation of the American Constitution and the issues and people who influenced it.

Peterson, Merrill D. *The Great Triumvirate: Webster, Clay, and Calhoun.* New York: Oxford, 1987. (H,A) Documents the individual lives and careers of these three men who impacted on the course of U.S. history during the first half of the 19th century.

Pick, Christopher. *Cities 2000.* New York: Facts on File, 1985. (J) Examines the history and growth of cities and provides ideas for solutions to urban problems.

Polmar, Norman. *Ships and Aircraft of the U.S. Fleet.* 14th ed. Annapolis, MD: Naval Institute, 1987. (H,A) Describes the U.S. Navy's current status.

Prange, Gordon W. *December 7, 1941: The Day the Japanese Attacked Pearl Harbor.* New York: McGraw-Hill, 1987. (H,A) Gives a chronological account of the attack on Pearl Harbor.

Pyle, Ernie. *Ernie's War: The Best of Ernie Pyle's World War II Dispatches.* New York: Random House, 1986. (H,A) A collection of Pyle's dispatches covering World War II from the Battle of Britain to the Pacific Campaigns.

R

Randall, Marta. *John F. Kennedy.* New York: Chelsea House, 1987. (M,J) Presents the life and times of Kennedy and covers all aspects of his presidency.

Randolph, Blythep. *Amelia Earhart*. New York: Watts, 1987. (J,H) Describes the life and career of this famous pilot from her girlhood to her mysterious disappearance.

Randolph, Sallie G. *Gerald R. Ford, President*. New York: Walker, 1987. (M,J) Discusses Ford's life and political career.

Reader's Digest. America's Historic Places: An Illustrated Guide to Our Country's Past. Westminster, MD: Reader's Digest, 1988. (H,A) Charts 500 sites nationwide that are of historical significance.

Rebel Voices: An IWW Anthology. Rev. ed. Chicago: Charles H. Kerr, 1988. (H,A) A collection of radical poems, songs, and cartoons about the Industrial Workers of the World.

Reflections on the Wall: The Vietnam Veterans Memorial. Harrisburg, PA: Stackpole, 1987. (H,A) Records events and formal ceremonies since 1982 honoring the memory of Vietnam veterans.

Reit, Seymour. *Behind Rebel Lines: The Incredible Story of Emma Edmonds, Civil War Spy*. New York: Harcourt Brace, 1988. (M,J) Relates the adventures of a woman who made eleven trips behind the rebel lines as a spy for the Union Army.

Remini, Robert V. *The Life of Andrew Jackson*. New York: Harper & Row, 1988. (H,A) Gives a well-researched analysis of the spirited man who was our seventh president.

Reynolds, Quentin James. *Custer's Last Stand*. New York: Random House, 1987. (M,J) A biography of the famous general who led the attack at the Battle of Little Big Horn.

Rhodes, Richard. *The Making of the Atomic Bomb*. New York: Simon & Schuster, 1986. (H,A) Traces the development of the atomic bomb from its concept to the bombing of Hiroshima.

Ride, Sally K. *To Space and Back*. New York: Lothrop, Lee & Shepard, 1986. (M,J) Describes a space journey from blast-off to landing, with examples of her own experiences.

Rinaldi, Ann. *Time Enough for Drums*. New York: Holiday House, 1986. (J) A young girl living in Trenton during the American Revolution matures as she learns about loyalty, patriotism, and love. F

Ripley, C. Peter. *Richard Nixon*. New York: Chelsea House, 1987. (M,J) Traces the life and career of Richard Nixon through his presidency.

Rummel, Jack. *Langston Hughes*. New York: Chelsea House, 1987. (J,H) Illustrates how Hughes's poetry and writing focused on his own race.

S

St. George, Judith. *The Mount Rushmore Story*. New York: Putnam, 1985. (J) Relates the life of Gutzon Borglum and his sculptures.

Sandak, Cass R. *Benjamin Franklin*. New York: Watts, 1986. (J) Covers Franklin's life from his boyhood to his major contributions to the growth of the country.

Sandburg, Carl. *Abe Lincoln Grows Up*. New York: Harcourt Brace, 1985. (M,J) Follows the life of Lincoln to the age of 19, when he travels to Illinois.

Sanders, Scott R. *Bad Man Ballad*. New York: Bradbury, 1986. (H) Seventeen-year-old Ely and a lawyer from Philadelphia make a dangerous trip into the Wilderness around Rome, Ohio, in 1912 in search of Bigfoot. F

Sapinsley, Barbara. *Taxes*. New York: Watts, 1986. A history of taxation in the U.S., including tax revolts and social security.

Scharf, Lois. *Eleanor Roosevelt: First Lady of American Liberalism*. Schenectady, NY: Twayne, 1987. (H,A) Discusses the life of Eleanor Roosevelt, her social reforms, and her role in American politics.

Schlesinger, Arthur. *The Cycles of American History*. Boston, Houghton Mifflin, 1986. (H,A) Explains how the values of one generation can influence public policies and the electorate 30 years later.

Schulke, Flip, and Penelope Ortner McPhee. *King Remembered*. New York: Norton, 1986. (H,A) Illustrates the life of Martin Luther King, Jr. and shows the history of the civil rights movement.

Schultz, Duane. *The Doolittle Raid*. New York: St. Martin's, 1988. (H,A) Describes the raid on Japan in April 1942—America's first strike against Japan.

Shenkman, Richard. *Legends, Lies, and Cherished Myths of American History*. New York: Morrow, 1988. (H,A) Debunks many myths of U.S history, from the founding fathers to the Reagan administration.

Shorto, Russell. *Geronimo*. Englewood Cliffs, NJ: Silver Burdett, 1989. (J,M,H) An illustrated biography of the Apache leader, focusing on his battles with Americans and Mexicans to reclaim the Apache homeland.

Shorto, Russell. *Tecumseh*. Englewood Cliffs, NJ: Silver Burdett, 1989. (J,M,H) Profiles the Shawnee chief and his attempts to secure an Indian nation.

Sifakis, Stewart. *Who Was Who in the Civil War*. New York: Facts on File, 1989. (J,H,A) Presents biographies of more than 2,500 people from the Civil war era, including generals, spies, writers, and politicians.

Smith, Barbara Clark. *After the Revolution: The Smithsonian History of Everyday Life in the Eighteenth Century*. New York: Pantheon, 1985. (H,A) Describes the earliest periods of American history through the lives of five actual 18th-century families.

Smith, Betsy Covington. *Jimmy Carter, President*. New York: Walker, 1986. (J) Profiles Carter's life from boyhood through his political years.

Smith, Betsy Covington. *Women Win the Vote*. Englewood Cliffs, NJ: Silver Burdett, 1989. (J,H) An illustrated history of the events that led to the ratification of the Nineteenth Amendment.

Smith, Carter, III. *One Giant Leap for Mankind*. Englewood Cliffs, NJ: Silver Burdett, 1986. (J,M,H) Follows the 1969 flight of Apollo 11, showing how the moon landing ushered in a new era in space.

Smith, Elizabeth Simpson. *Five First Ladies: A Look Into the Lives of Nancy Reagan, Rosalynn Carter, Betty Ford, Pat Nixon, and Lady Bird Johnson*. New York: Walker, 1986. (J) Describes the duties of the President's wife, focusing on these five First Ladies.

Smith, Howard E. *Daring the Unknown: A History of NASA*. New York: Harcourt Brace, 1987. (J,M) Recounts the history of NASA and its accomplishments.

Smith, Howard E. *Disarmament: The Road to Peace*. Englewood Cliffs, NJ: Julian Messner, 1986. (J,M) A comprehensive look at the nuclear age: its background, the arms race, and the prospects for disarmament and world peace.

Smith, Page. *The Rise of Industrial America: A People's History of the Post-Reconstruction Era*. New York: McGraw-Hill, 1984. (H,A) This history of the U.S. between 1876 and 1901 focuses on new scientific ideas and the conflicts between business and labor.

Sobel, Robert. *Panic on Wall Street: A Classic History of America's Financial Disasters*. Rev. ed. New York: Dutton, 1988. (H,A) Profiles financial disasters from William Duer's 1792 collapse to Wall Street's plunge in October 1987.

Staten, Jay, and Pat Staten. *The Embattled Farmer*. Golden, CO: Fulcrum, 1987. (H,A) Summarizes 20th-century economic and government programs that affect the American family farmer.

Stern, Alan. *The U.S. Space Program After Challenger: Where Are We Going?* New York: Watts, 1987. (J) Discusses the Challenger accident, the future of the American space program, and the possible commercialization of space.

Sullivan, George. *Ronald Reagan*. New York: Julian Messner, 1985. (J,H) Examines the life of Ronald Reagan from boyhood to the presidency.

T

Tapert, Annette, ed. *Lines of Battle: Letters from U.S. Servicemen, 1941–1945*. New York: Times Books, 1987. (H,A) A collection of letters from all types and ranks of American soldiers.

Terkel, Studs. *Working*. New York: Ballantine, 1985. (H,A) Based on personal accounts, this look at 20th-century work ethics and habits crosses class boundaries.

Terris, Susan. *Nell's Quilt*. New York: Farrar Straus, 1987. (H) Eighteen-year-old Nell wants to work for the women's suffrage movement but is trapped by her responsibilities on the farm. F

This Fabulous Century: Sixty Years of American Life. Alexandria, VA: Time-Life, 1969–. (J,H,A) A pictorial history of American civilization from 1900 to 1970.

Tiede, Tom. *American Tapestry: Eyewitness Accounts of the Twentieth Century*. New York: Pharos, 1988. (H,A) Introduces the era through the recollections of people born near 1900.

Tuchman, Barbara W. *The First Salute*. New York: Knopf, 1988. (H,A) Views the American revolution within the European context.

Tucker, Patrick T. *Riding the High Country*. Seattle, WA: Fjord, 1987. (H,A) Relates the friendship of the author and the artist Charles M. Russell and presents the story of early Montana.

Turner, Ann. *Third Girl from the Left*. New York: Macmillan, 1986. (J,H) Sarah leaves her home in 19th-century Maine to become the mail-order bride of a Montana rancher.

U

Utley, Robert M. *Cavalier in Buckskin: George Armstrong Custer and the Western Military Frontier*. Norman, OK: University of Oklahoma Press, 1988. (H,A) A definitve biography that describes a complex man and the U.S. war on the Plains Indians.

W

Wade, Wyn Craig. *The Fiery Cross: The Ku Klux Klan in America*. New York: Simon & Schuster, 1987. (H,A) A history of the development of the Ku Klux Klan.

Waldman, Carl. *Atlas of the North American Indian*. New York: Facts on File, 1985. (J,H,A) Traces the history, cultures, migrations, and wars of the major North American tribes.

Waldman, Carl. *Encyclopedia of the Native American Tribes*. New York: Facts on File, 1988. (J,H,A) Describes the history, culture, life, and conflicts of 150 North American tribes.

Weatherford, Doris. *Foreign and Female: Immigrant Women in America, 1840-1940*. New York: Schocken, 1987. (H,A) Chronicles the plight of immigrant women from 1840 to 1940, focusing on religion, family life, marriage, and work.

Webb, Shayann, and Rachel West Nelson. *Selma, Lord, Selma: Girlhood Memories of the Civil Rights Days*. Tuscaloosa, AL: University of Alabama Press, 1980. (H,A) Recounts the events of the 1965 civil rights movement in Selma, Alabama, through the eyes of two who were girls at the time.

Weidhorn, Manfred. *Robert E. Lee*. New York: Atheneum, 1988. (M,J) Focuses on Lee and the Civil War amd analyzes Lee's role.

Welch, James. *Fools Crow*. New York: Viking, 1986. (H,A) The Pikuni Indians of Montana are forced to choose between war or surrender as the westward movement of whites threatens their existence.

Westerfeld, Scott. *The Berlin Airlift*. Englewood Cliffs, NJ: Silver Burdett, 1989. (J,M,H) Chronicles and illustrates the U.S. mandate to counteract the Soviet blockade and its impact on the burgeoning cold war.

Willenson, Kim, et al. *The Bad War: An Oral History of the Vietnam War*. (New York: NAL, 1987. (H,A) Examines America's political and military role in Vietnam.

Williams, Earl P. *What You Should Know About the American Flag*. Lanham, MD: Maryland Historical Press, 1987. (M,J) A comprehensive guide to the history and traditions of Old Glory.

Williams, John Hoyt. *A Great Shining Road: The Epic Story of the Transcontinental Railroad*. New York: Times Books, 1988. (H) A history of the building of the railroad, including biographical accounts.

Wills, Charles. *The Tet Offensive*. Englewood Cliffs, NJ: Silver Burdett, 1989. (J,M,H) Describes U.S. involvement in Vietnam, focusing on the Tet Offensive.

Woods, Harold, and Geraldine Woods. *The United Nations*. New York: Watts, 1985. (M,J) Describes the history, goals, organization, and specialized agencies of the UN and the world problems it encounters.

Worth, Richard. *You'll Be Old Someday, Too*. New York: Watts, 1986. (J) Discusses current and historical attitudes toward the aging and their lifestyle and problems.

Wright, Lawrence. *In the New World: Growing Up with America, 1960-1984*. New York: Knopf, 1988. (H,A) A biographical account of living through the cultural, political, and social change of these 25 years.

Wright, Richard. *Native Son*. New York: NAL, 1961. (J,M,H) A young boy's journey to manhood in the South teaches him hard but valuable lessons about racial, social, and economic prejudice. F

Writing Red: An Anthology of American Women Writers, 1930-1940. New York: Feminist Press, 1988. (H,A) Collects short stories, poems, and journalism by female radicals of the 1930s.

Y

Yeager, Jeana, and Dick Rutan. *Voyager*. New York: Knopf, 1987. (H,A) Tells the story behind the flight that set the record for circling the world without refueling.

Betty H. Grebey is Library Coordinator, Downington Area School District, Downington, Pennsylvania, and Lecturer in the Graduate School of Library Science, Villanova University. She is an active member of the American Library Association, the American Association of School Librarians, and the Pennsylvania Shool Librarians Association. Ms. Grebey was a member of the CIP Advisory Committee for the Library of Congress and is now chairperson of the Baker & Taylor *School Selection Guide* Committee.

The editors of the updated edition of the *American Heritage Illustrated History of the United States* are particularly grateful for the assistance of the following individuals and institutions in the editorial development of the new volumes.

Cynthia Crippen, Felice Levy, AEIOU Inc.; American Telephone & Telegraph Company; Jeanne Bristol, Henry Burr, Gene Lane, Wendy James, Americomp; Apple Computer; Avnet, Inc.; Bantam Books; British Information Services; The Brooklyn Public Library; The George Bush for President Campaign Committee; Martin I. Elze, The Jimmy Carter Library; Harold Nash, David Napell, Pascal Perri, Robert H. Rosen, Lynn Sherinski, Shelley Wayne, Choice Publishing, Inc.; Ann Hughes, Christies; Jay Price, Commission on the Bicentennial of the United States Constitution; Jerry Johnson, Department of Defense; The District of Columbia Public Library; The Robert Dole for President Campaign Committee; Martin M. Teasley, The Dwight D. Eisenhower Library; Eleanora Schoenebaum, Facts-On-File Publishing Co.; Richard L. Holzhausen, The Gerald R. Ford Library; Kim Adler, The Ford Motor Company; Katherine M. Hopper, the Hirschhorn Museum and Sculpture Garden/Smithsonian Institution; Jessie O. Kempter, I.B.M.; The International Ladies' Garment Workers Union; E. Philip Scott, The Lyndon B. Johnson Library; James M. Cedrone, The John F. Kennedy Library; The Library of Congress; Judy Wheeler, Lockheed Corporation; Movie Star News; Peter Humphrey, N.A.S.A.; The National Baseball Library; The New York Coalition for the Homeless; The New York Historical Society; The New York Public Library; The National Archives; The National Portrait Gallery; James Hastings, The Nixon Project; The Polaroid Corporation; Frank Thomas, U.S. Postal Service; James Hintz, Kim Storbakken, Judith Welling, R. R. Donnelley & Sons Co.; The U.S. Surgeon General's Office; The United States Supreme Court; Tone Graphics; The U.S. Department of Transportation; Benedict K. Sobrist, The Harry S. Truman Library; The United Nations; Elizabeth Ingoldsby, United Technology; Kit Melick and Frank Topper, *The Wall Street Journal;* Nat Andriani, Wide World Photos; The White House; Gao Xuega, Xinhua News Agency.

Richard Eastman, Whitney Ellsworth, Scott Ferguson, Gertrude Arlene Goldberg, Anne Hardgrove, Lorna Harris, Judy Knipe, Donald Kobler, Barbara Marks, Robyn O'Connor, Kevin Osborn, Peter Pettus, Elizabeth Prince, William Schwartz, David Scott, John Shanks, Betsy Smith, Sunny Sit, Sally Vagliano, Evelyn Vogel, Charles Wills, Ellen Wilson.